The Writer's Friend

Behind the Scenes with Editors

By Linda Davis Kyle, Joseph Gregg, and Nancy McAlary

Foreword By Ron Franscell

Editor's Note By Guy Lancaster

Linda Davis Kyle

First Edition

WritingNow.com Publishing
Austin, Texas

Compliments of Barbara Litterington

Manufactured in the United States of America by Great Impressions, Dallas, TX

Cover Design: Image Express, Austin, TX

First Printing: March 2000

WritingNow.com Publishing • P.O. Box 270070 • Austin, TX 78727 USA • 512.837.7683

Library of Congress Catalog Card Number: ~~94-12045~~ LCCN: 99-96848

Publisher's Cataloging In Publication
   (Provided by Quality Books, Inc.)

Kyle, Linda Davis.
    The writer's friend: behind the scenes with
   editors / by Linda Davis Kyle, Joseph Gregg, and
   Nancy McAlary ; foreword by Ron Franscell ;
   editor's note by Guy Lancaster — 1st. ed.
       p. cm.
   Includes bibliographical references and index.
    ~~LCCN: 94-12045~~ LCCN: 99-96848
    ISBN: 0-9673651-0-4

    1. Authorship—Handbooks, manuals, etc.
   2. Authors and publishers. 3. Authorship—Marketing.
   I. Gregg, Joseph. II. McAlary, Nancy.
   III. Title.

PN151.K95 2000   808'.02
                                QBI99-1736

Dedication

To Professors Robert Bode, Homer Kemp, Alan Slotkin, and
Albert Wilhelm at Tennessee Technological University.

Table of Contents

Index

Acknowledgements

I am grateful to Ron Franscell, Editor of the *News-Record* and author of *Angel Fire* and *The Deadline,* for his Foreword and contributions, to Joseph Gregg, author of *Write Your Way to Riches*, for his guest chapter, and to Lynn Grisard Fullman, Southeast Tourism Society's Travel Writer of the Year and author of *Fun with the Family in Alabama*, for her critique and contributions. I also appreciate the input from other award-winning writers Dan Auiler, Liz Carpenter, Sonia Pressman Fuentes, Margaret McAlister, Fern Michaels, Robert Powers, Shara Rendell-Smock, and Robert J. Sawyer.

I am honored by the kindness of Renu Aldrich, Public Relations Manager of PR Newswire, Dan Forbush, President of ProfNet and Vice-President of Media Relations for PR Newswire, Lynn Davidson, Senior Account Executive at R.R. Bowker, and Yoichi Arakawa, President of Six Strings Music Publishing. I acknowledge Mike Sedge of Strawberry Media and graphic artist Elizabeth Lary for their interest in this book and ASJA Administrative Assistant Heather Vanarsdel for supplying information. I am thankful to FCL, LWCB, MB, and OQB librarians of the Austin Public Library System and to the reference librarians of the Perry Castañeda Library at the University of Texas.

I am sustained by the work of Guy Lancaster, editor of *The Writer's Friend*, the layout and cover design, critique, and contributions of Ralph S. Marston, Jr., of Image Express, Inc., and the technical expertise and generosity of Della Newman and Severiano Gonzales of Speedy's Printing.

I am supported by my friend, Nancy McAlary, an internationally published writer of Brisbane, Australia, for co-authoring our vignette, "A Day in the Life of an Editor," my writer friends, Ray Bronk, Mike Everman, Bill Spencer, and the Austin Writers' League.

I am mindful of Carol Crutchfield, Jean Garlick, Don and Donna Goertz, John Green, John Henderson, Jean-Pierre and Nickla Heudier, Mahboob Hossain, Gerard Luna, Robert Martindale, Dora Montante, Doug Phelan, Bonnie Rathmell, Sr. Corona Sharp, and Vicky Tanguma for their good wishes. I am fostered by Homer and Carol Davis, Ernestine Hoffmann, Edna Qualls, and Marie Qualls.

I am embraced by the encouragement of Mildred, Reba, Rich, Brock, Brett, and Ivana Kyle. I am indebted particularly to Brock, the creator and webmaster of *WritingNow.com,* from which this book grew, for his support and many hours of work.

Finally, I am appreciative to the many editors, publishers, and media specialists who helped to make *The Writer's Friend—Behind the Scenes with Editors* a reality.

Angela Adair-Hoy, Publisher, *The Write Markets Report*, Andover, MA

Jim Adair, Editor, *Homes & Cottages*, Mississauga, Ontario, Canada

Renu Aldrich, Public Relations Manager, PR NewsWire, New York, NY

G.W. Amick, Editor, *The First Word Bulletin*, Madrid, Spain

Ken Beaulieu, Executive Editor, *Continental*, Boston, MA

Judi Becker, Editor, *CATsumer Report* and *Good Dog!*, Austin, TX

Denise Castañon, Former Managing Editor, *Estylo* Magazine,
   Los Angeles, CA (Linda F. Cauthen, Current Managing Editor)

Joanne Cosker, Assistant Editor, *The Educated Traveler*, Chantilly, VA

Anthony Mark Dalessandro, Former Editor, *Italian America*,
   Washington, DC (Brenda Dalessandro, Current Editor)

Scott Edelman, Editor of *Sci-Fi Entertainment*, Reston, VA

James Floto, Editor/Publisher, *The Diamond Angle*, Kihei, HI

Dan Forbush, President, ProfNet and Vice-President of Media Relations,
   NEWSdesk, Long Island, NY

Ron Franscell, Editor, *News-Record*, Gillette, WY

Sara Gilbert, Editor, *U.S. Art*, Minneapolis, MN

Paul Grogan, Deputy Editor, *Global Adventure*, London, England, UK

Gena Holle, Editor & Owen C. Hardy, Publisher, *International Railway
   Traveler*, San Diego, CA

Tim Horan, Managing Editor, *The Greyhound Review*, Abilene, KS

Howard Jardine, Editor, *Balance Fitness*, London, England, UK

Greg Jones, Editor, *Sailing* Magazine, Port Washington, WI

Robert Joseph, Editor, *Weekend Woodcrafts*, Concord, CA

Mark Kalan, Editor, *CC Motorcycle NewsMagazine*, Nyack, NY

Anne Kennedy, *The Silver Web*, Tallahassee, FL

Guy Lancaster, Editorial Assistant, *The Arkansas Review:
   A Journal of Delta Studies*, Jonesboro, AR

Julia Bencomo Lobaco, Editor, *Vista Magazine,* Coral Gables, FL

Wendy McCallum, Co-Editor, *Healthy Options*, Tauranga, New Zealand

Karen Menehan, Editor, *Massage Magazine*, Santa Cruz, CA

Debbie Ridpath Ohi, Editor, *Inklings*, Toronto, Ontario, Canada

Harold Ort, Editor, *Popular Communications*, Hicksville, NY

Robert Powers, Copy Editor, Andover News Service, Greater Boston, MA

Kathryn Ptacek, Publisher, *Gila Queen's Guide to Markets*, Newton, NJ

Vanessa Raphaely, Editor, *Cosmopolitan*, Cape Town, South Africa

David P. Robson, Former Editor, *Chem Matters*, Washington, DC

Lisa Rosenthal, Editor, *San Francisco Peninsula Parent*, San Francisco, CA

Carol Schaal, Managing Editor, *Notre Dame Magazine*, Notre Dame, IN

Chad Schlegel, Managing Editor *Great Lakes Angler* and *Lakeland Boating*, Evanston, IL

Joseph Sherman, Former Editor, *Jewish Affairs*, Johannesburg, South Africa

Andy Sperandeo, Editor, *Model Railroader*, Waukesha, WI

Ed Starkie, Website Coordinator, *BodyIsland*, Ashburton, Devon, UK

Robert N. Stephenson, Editor, *Altair*, Blackwood, SA, Australia

Anne Tullis, Editor, *Bahrain Gateway*, *Golden Falcon*, *Oryx*, and *Oryx— Entertainment*, Manama, Bahrain

M.J. Van Deventer, Editor, *Persimmon Hill*, Oklahoma City, OK

Donna Welsh, Production Editor, *WellBeing*, Sydney, NSW, Australia

Jan Werblin, Associate Editor, *Professional Counselor Magazine*, Deerfield Beach, FL

Peter Wrobel, Editorial Manager, *Nature*, London, England, UK

Foreword

Plenty of publishing pundits will tell you a writer has no friends in this business.

Yes, there are lots of friendly people out there—agents, editors, publicists, publishers, distributors, and booksellers—but each has a profit motive for chumming up to the source of their raw material: You. The good old days when brilliant editors nurtured writers and their careers in a literary Garden of Eden are over. This is a time when gigantic, hulking, corporate reptiles prowl the publishing landscape. Go ahead, name one renowned editor. Max Perkins is dead. Long live the nameless, faceless mercantilists!

The fact is that some of these people are truly friendly, and *all* of them are vital to your success as a writer. Each brings a unique talent or knowledge to your team. Knowing how they think and what arouses their own creative juices—and understanding how your artistic and business interests can blend—will give you an edge over all those writers who skulk around in an "us versus them" funk. They are on a collision course to an eventual calamity with the publishing industry.

It's helpful to think of yourself as crucial to the process, but not indispensable. For every byline in every national magazine today, there are 100 hungry, but capable, writers who would split their mother's infinitive to be published. Editors know this, and, like you, they will take the path of least resistance if it still leads to their ultimate destination: Publication and profit.

So maybe a writer doesn't have many true friends in the publishing business, but you won't succeed if you have enemies created by a flimsy grasp of the business. It is perfectly natural, even necessary, that you think like an artist while you translate magic from your mind to the page, but when you emerge from your lonely garret, you must also think like a merchant. You must assess the commercial quality of your product, study its market, and put it where somebody will buy it.

The Writer's Friend is a treasure trove of practical advice. It provides some excellent thoughts about how you can become a team player, even the team captain, in getting published. And to get published, you'll need a good team.

It's a good rule for writing, and maybe a good rule for life: Try to understand the other guy. If you do, your art will blossom and maybe, finally, somebody will try to see things your way, too.

Ron Franscell
Editor, *News-Record*, Gillette, WY
Author, *Angel Fire* and *The Deadline*

About the Authors

Linda Davis Kyle

Linda Davis Kyle has written hundreds of articles on health, fitness, and nutrition, martial arts and other sports, automotive care, pets, parenting, and safety. She wrote a monthly health column for a Texas magazine and a British e-zine for over two years and a weekly general interest column for a Tennessee newspaper for almost three years. Her articles have been published in Canada, the United States, the Netherlands Antilles, Ireland, England, South Africa, Bahrain, Bangladesh, Japan, and Australia in publications such as *Chem Matters*, *Martial Arts Training*, *Golden Falcon*, *WellBeing,* and *World Travel Magazine.*

Kyle especially has addressed the positive affects of good nutrition on the health of the eyes and the health of the athlete. She served on the board of directors of Prevent Blindness for nine years and also has contributed over 500 hours service at Recording for the Blind. She has demonstrated her devotion to fitness by winning national karate championships, receiving All American Awards, and earning a black belt in Shito-Ryu.

She earned her M.A. in English from Tennessee Technological University. She was an editor for *The Journal of Chemical Education* for 18 years. Kyle teaches an informal class in writing at the University of Texas.

Joseph Gregg

Joseph Gregg has worked as a contract technical writer, web designer, and software tester for eight years. His major clients have included Houghton Mifflin Company, Fidelity Investments, State Street Bank and Trust, State Street Global Advisors, and Aspect Development.

He is the author of *Write Your Way to Riches*, which shows individuals how to break into the lucrative field of technical writing. Information on his book can be found at writeformoney.hypermart.net.

An avid investor, he also serves on the board of directors of Steep, a company that makes and sells gourmet teas and cocoas.

Gregg earned a degree in animal science from Cornell University in 1989 and received a certificate in technical writing from the University of Massachusetts at Lowell in 1993.

Nancy McAlary

Nancy McAlary began writing creative fiction in 1996, and since that time her short fiction has been published in magazines worldwide, including Australia, New Zealand, South Africa, the United Kingdom, and the United States.

She is a native of Canada and received her B.A. degree from Trent University in Peterborough, Ontario. She also was granted a diploma in horticulture and has been employed in a variety of positions, which have supplied "fodder" for her creative imagination.

McAlary has lived in Australia for the past 12 years where she and her husband, Richard, own and operate a computer company. Her passions include growing native Australian plants and encouraging wildlife back into the suburban backyard.

Chapter 1.
Finding Encouragement

If it has been your dream to write and to be published, yet you have had no one to support you, *The Writer's Friend: Behind the Scenes with Editors* is for you. It is my goal to help steer you away from calamities with editors. The step-by-step basics that I share about dealing with editors can help you to receive your first byline and to develop as the writer you aspire to be.

If you have been published in national magazines and would like to begin querying and submitting to international publications, this book can guide you, too.

TWF is perhaps *the first* book to show how magazine editors view writers and how editors would like writers to change. More than 40 editors from Canada, the United States, the United Kingdom, Spain, South Africa, Bahrain, Australia, and New Zealand have confirmed the need for this book and have explained what writers must know and do to succeed. While I have paraphrased some of their materials to prevent the creation of a mere chain of quotations, I have shared verbatim much of what the editors report to unveil their passion for the writing profession and to point out their expectations.

In addition, authors Dan Auiler, Liz Carpenter, Ron Franscell, Sonia Pressman Fuentes, Lynn Grisard Fullman, Ralph Marston, Margaret McAlister, Fern Michaels, Robert Powers, Shara Rendell-Smock, and Robert J. Sawyer offer power-packed suggestions about the craft of writing and penetrating the publishing industry.

Having edited well over 4000 typescripts during my 18 years as an editor for *The Journal of Chemical Education* and having been a freelance editor and writer, I have seen the world of writing through the eyes of an editor and a writer. Along with a plethora of tips from editors and writers throughout the book, I also have included hints of my own and questions to direct you. The fundamental approach to writing and publishing presented here is only one of many. Use from this book what wins sales for you. It is my dream that this book will enhance your creativity and increase your productivity.

Together, Australian writer Nancy McAlary and I "put you in an editor's shoes" with our vignette, "A Day in the Life of an Editor," and McAlary shares some of her hints for writing short fiction. Technical writer Joseph Gregg—author of *Write Your Way to Riches*—introduces the lucrative world of technical writing in "Chapter 18. Finding out about Editors, Employment Agencies, and Technical Writers."

For your convenience, I have collected and presented the questions from the chapters in an appendix. In addition, I provide an index to make the book a handy reference.

The cumulative power from 20 rapid-read chapters can help you to build profitable relationships with editors and publishers. Like a lighthouse, *The Writer's Friend*, with its guidance from editors around the world, illuminates your way through mighty tempests to safe and cordial harbors.

With each reading of *TWF*, I hope that new facets will emerge to help you when you need them most and are ready to receive the ideas.

Encouraging You

If you sometimes feel that you are a writer who has been overlooked in the shuffle, just know that with your continued hard work, discipline, and perseverance, your genuine and heartfelt words can be published more and more frequently. Your impact as a writer may be greater than you imagine, so never give up your dream. If writing is what you want to do, then no matter what anyone says to try to dissuade you or what anyone does to put obstacles in your path, keep studying and reading and working to improve your craft. If you can relate to Lawrence Clark Powell's words in Jessamyn West's *Hide and Seek* that "Writing is a solitary occupation. Family, friends, and society are the natural enemies of a writer. [A writer] must be alone, uninterrupted and slightly savage [in order] to sustain and complete an undertaking," *TWF* can empower you.

It is my genuine goal in writing this book to help you achieve your mission to be published, to be published more consistently, to extend your horizons and your possibilities, and to increase your earning power. Be inspired by the Chinese proverb, "First resolve what must be done; solutions will then become evident." *The Writer's Friend* can be there every step of the way, encouraging and championing you when times seem bleak and congratulating you as you win assignment after assignment from the many editors to whom you submit your finest queries and best writings. When you conquer your fears, sharpen your skills, set your goals, and work to achieve your goals in an atmosphere of positive expectations, you can succeed.

Happy writing!

• • •

Chapter 2. Getting on the Right Track

If you're shopping for an elegant piece of jewelry, you don't hike to a lumberyard for such a purchase. If you want to enjoy a Chinese dinner, you don't drive to the nearest Mexican restaurant. If you're planning a dinner party for a dozen guests, you won't open the nearest phone book, glide your finger down the page and invite random people. Similarly, if you write a query or an article about horses, you would submit neither the idea nor the typescript to a publication whose focus is homes or motorcycles or railway history or sailing or art.

Or would you?

Upon careful study, the seemingly unsuitable and zany market possibilities for articles pertaining to horses might not be a waste of time. Be open to new possibilities and bold ideas. At the same time, be logical. If the homes magazine presents estates that boast luxuries such as tennis courts, swimming pools, spas, and stables, you potentially could land a sale if the editor actually would like an article on, let's say, "Stables for the Modern Horse."

You could include a section on today's special stall floor systems designed to provide safe footing, reduce moisture and ammonia vapor, and minimize bacteria. From there you could discuss mesh panel stalls and classic wood stalls, hinged Dutch doors, and door guards. You could include up-to-the-minute information on heavy duty stall mats, cast aluminum feeders, swing out hay and grain feeders, and always fresh "horse waterers." You could go on from there to discuss stable accessories such as saddle racks, blankets, halters, tack and even personal items for the pampered horse such as "designer hoods and shoulder guards that let your horse say goodnight to messy manes, shoulder irritation, and chafing." The editor might even change the title to "Suites for the Modern Horse."

Your greatest challenge with your "Suite for Equines" article will be to write it in a manner that gives the information without turning it into an advertisement for all these modern wonders that horses can enjoy. The lines of demarcation in magazines between articles and advertisements are quite clear with some. Yet, some others may be a bit blurry to you. If there are no ads for equine paraphernalia in your target magazine, then you can write your article free from any feeling of entanglement with advertising. You cannot be accused of plugging any products, especially because you will not name products but rather you will introduce, describe, and evaluate them for the convenience and benefit of your readers.

Knowing about Pegs

From another side of the coin, a publication that would be interested in such an article, whether it had accompanying ads or not, probably would run such an article to coincide with some upcoming equine event.

An American editor might like to run the article in May to synchronize with the Kentucky Derby or in August to line up with the Tennessee Walking Horse National Celebration. A Canadian editor might like to run the article in August to match up with the Royal Red Arabian Horse Show. A British editor could find it an appealing article to run in May at the time of the Royal Windsor Horse Show. You get the picture. The topic is teeming with special publication pegs. Remember, though, customize the article for each editor's publication. Do not send a form query or a form article.

Using Pegs to Expand Your Chances of Publication

To help you find pegs to suggest for your articles, you will appreciate the annual publication *Chase's* (current year) *Calendar of Events*. If you are writing about a famous person in history, you can peg your project around the anniversary of the celebrity's date of birth or death and submit your query or article well in advance to meet the magazine's lead time. If you prepare an article on women's health care, you could mention to the editor that you can have it ready for use in May during Women's Health Care Month. If you are planning to write "The Fun of Learning to Play the Guitar," you can offer the article for use in April to mesh with International Guitar Month. If your interest centers on automobiles, and you want to write an article on "How to Recognize a Great Automotive Technician," you might peg your article for publication in October to correspond with Car Care Month. *Chase's Calendar of Events* offers a seemingly endless supply of pegs for your articles.

Sometimes your editor will tell you that she has found a peg for your article. In July 1998, Carmen Keltner —former Editor of the *Austin Writer*, the newsletter of the Austin Writers' League—wrote to me to say that she would be running my article, "Finding Encouragement," in her August edition of the *Austin Writer*. She said, "It ties in beautifully with the forthcoming agents conference because you give such good advice."

Using Pegs with Caution

You, of course, can mention the potential peg to your editor. You need not mention the events, per se, in your articles. Your articles merely need to be in phase with the events to support their time frames.

If you write on an event such as Breaux Bridge Crawfish Fest that is celebrated in Breaux Bridge, Louisiana, in May every year, then you significantly limit the use of your article. If you query and your editor wants an article on the Breaux Bridge Crawfish Fest, then that is fine. You mention pegs to expand your opportunities, not to limit them. So, offer pegs with great care.

Checking Many Angles

Most likely a motorcycle magazine would have nothing to say about horses, but just suppose the editor of the motorcycle magazine is a history buff. Suppose she runs a mini-history column each month. You study a dozen back issues and the most current issue and see that all those history columns have been definitions of words to enlighten her readers. Now you see that you actually could query with your idea—"The Etymology of Horsepower"— and explain that you feel it can fit her unique history column. The fact that other motorcycle magazines are not suitable for such a piece is excellent. You can be assured that she knows that her competitors do not run such a column. So, automatically, she knows that you have done your homework. You are on the same wavelength with her. You are offering a viable piece for her history column. No doubt, you have an extra high chance to land this sale and potentially many others.

Next you study your huge stack of railway magazines and also research how horses have been shipped through the ages. Then you know whether or not you should query with "Shipping Stallions by Railway."

Blush-faced, you wonder how you possibly could have thought of submitting a query about horses to a sailing magazine. Then you locate an article that the editor published over a year ago called "Horses Lost at Sea." You study more issues to decide whether your fresh idea has merit or must you continue your search for a suitable market or change your topic or change your angle of approach.

Then you study issue after issue of the art magazine that has enchanted you to see if you can complement its materials. Suddenly you find that two years ago, the editor ran an article on "Cowboys and their Horses"—an art exhibit in Santa Fe, New Mexico. Voila! Now you think you might submit your query on "Appaloosas Captured on Canvas."

Noting Special Qualifications Required

Finally, you find an equine magazine that needs articles on caring for your horse, which is where you began your search with your initial idea of "Keeping Your Horse Healthy." The catch is that the authors of the health articles for this particular equine magazine must be qualified veterinarians. Many magazines require that the authors be qualified practitioners of their trade or profession and be steeped in their subject matter with years of experience with their topics.

Go back to your search for an equine magazine that welcomes writers who can supplement their knowledge with research and interviews. You persevere and find another possibility. Yes. This equine magazine invites writers to interview busy veterinarians to collect their up-to-the-minute ideas on horse health, do the write-up with the utmost care, and document library, online, and live sources.

Clarifying Your Candidacy

Being properly informed is a must. Because many publications do not accept articles from professional writers, just studying your target magazine is not enough.

Even if your writing is enchanting and award-winning, it may not be in the contest for some publications. Peter Wrobel, Editorial Manager of the prestigious journal, *Nature*, published in London, England, does not generally publish unsolicited contributions from professional writers. Regarding scientists writing about their own original research, what Wrobel looks for most—apart from the quality of the research itself—is "a clear and simply written explanation of why the article might appeal to a broad scientific readership."

While some publications want only those writers who live and breathe their topic of choice, many others welcome well-researched topics. You merely must ferret out the magazines that are right for you. Order writer's guidelines, if they are available, to help you make sure that you are eligible to submit queries and articles to your target magazine. Study and follow the instructions that the editors have detailed. Then look for bold twists to excite their interests and land assignments.

If your annual *Writer's Market*, the grandfather of all U.S. market guides, says that your target magazine will send writer's guidelines, either free or for a price, always order them. It cannot be overemphasized that these contributor's guidelines spell out many important instructions that, if followed precisely, place the astute writer ahead of those who choose to be careless competitors in the writing game. Among other significant pieces of advice, these guidelines will let you know if the publishers require queries or if they prefer full typescript submissions. The guidelines will inform you of their e-mail policies. Guidelines properly used are like having a special invitation to a party. You know whether you should rent formal garb or wear shorts and carry along your swimwear.

As you navigate the internet and find listings of magazines and e-zines that are seeking writers, always respectfully contact these editors to ask for their writer's guidelines, as well. Never submit articles by e-mail to publishers until you know their e-mail submission policies and whether they prefer typescripts sent in the body of an e-mail message or as an attachment.

Following an Editor's Special Instructions

So you may be thinking that the article that you are proposing is so wonderful that you can slide it across home base to a victorious home run for yourself [your team of one] without following the publication's requirements. Your work may be good. It may be great. However, calling attention to yourself in violation of an editor's preferences more likely will put you out of the game. Always take writer's guidelines seriously. They are one of your most important maps. M.J. Van Deventer, the Editor of *Persimmon Hill* magazine and Director of Publications, National Cowboy Hall of Fame and Western Heritage Center, Oklahoma City, Oklahoma, says, "It needs to be obvious that writers have studied my publication and our guidelines by adhering to the suggestions in the guidelines." Reflect on the import of Van Deventer's words. This vital information cannot be overemphasized. Think carefully about what she is saying. Adhere to her suggestion if you want to win assignments, publish consistently, and increase your earnings.

Determining the Percentage of Articles Open

After you have determined your eligibility, then you need to see how open your target publication is to freelance writers. Compare current masthead names with the bylines to determine the percentage of articles supplied by freelance writers in your target magazine. Do staff names fill only a couple of bylines? If so, your chances are good if you query politely with a dynamite topic that you can compose and deliver on time.

In addition, refer to the most up-to-date *Writer's Market*. It may tell you that your target publication is 90 or even 100 percent freelance written.

Accommodating Editorial Calendars

If the editors of your target magazines share their editorial calendars with writers, request them politely and use their calendars wisely to accommodate their needs.

Ken Beaulieu, the Executive Editor of *Continental*, Boston, Massachusetts, who shares his editorial calendar with writers, says,

> If a writer truly wants to contribute to *Continental* magazine, persistence pays off. The first—and most important—step is to discuss the editorial calendar with me. Not only does it show enthusiasm on your part, it helps me get a feel for your strengths. If there is a particular story I believe is right up your alley, I would expect to see a rather detailed query within the next week. Barring any unforeseen problems or changes to the schedule, I will then make the formal assignment.

Some publications organize each issue around a particular theme. If your target publication organizes in such a fashion, and if the editorial staff shares its proposed plans with writers, you can focus queries and typescripts to accommodate those needs. If you submit a query, or a completed typescript—if that is what the editor prefers—well in advance of the stated deadline, you greatly increase the chances of your work being accepted.

Paying Attention to Details

If you pay attention to details and follow the instructions of the writer's guidelines of your target market, you will be well on the way to increasing your sales.

Ralph Marston, author of *The Daily Motivator,* says,

Anyone who thinks they're too important to be bothered by details will eventually be undermined by their own arrogance and ignorance. Details matter. Details are supremely important. Details are very much worth knowing about. Certainly you want to delegate tasks and responsibility when appropriate. Certainly you want to keep your eye on the "big picture." But don't neglect the details. Get the details right. Paying attention to details can make the difference between a losing team and one that wins the championship. Details can give your business a sizable competitive advantage, or they can put you out of business, depending on whether you attend to them or not. Dive into the details. Know them, respect their importance, and they can make all the difference in the world for you.

Studying Sample Copies from a Writer's Perspective

The best way to know whether an editor might welcome your query and your followup article is to track down and study several issues of your target magazine.

Making Only Selective Submissions

Regarding the extreme importance of making only selective submissions, think about the words of Jim Adair, Editor-in-Chief of *Homes & Gardens*: "Freelancers hate getting rejection form letters from editors, but guess what? Editors hate getting form letters from freelancers who are obviously pitching the same idea to dozens of publications, without regard to regional differences or to what the magazine covers."

The importance of submitting very individualized queries for the editors to whom you submit cannot be overemphasized. Remember, always make very selective submissions. Never, never send form queries to editors. Debbie Ridpath Ohi, the Editor of *Inklings*, a free biweekly newsletter for writers—

under the auspices of Inkspot—says, "I like writers who have bothered to look at back issues and the guidelines to get a feel for the kind of style and content I prefer. . . . But most of all, I like to see queries that are specific in focus and targeted directly at my publication."

Submitting to Noncompeting Publications

Remember, even if you choose to deal with magazine editors who allow simultaneous queries, be courteous to them and be kind to yourself. Never submit the same query to publications that are direct competitors. If you decide to query competitors, slant your query and your article uniquely for each magazine. Some of the same research and interview materials may be useful, but make sure that your queries have very different slants. Dealing with direct competitors can be like playing with fire. While some may embrace you even though their competitor has published your work, some others may not. So map out a safe and sensible marketing strategy.

In researching and interviewing for information on ways to keep a healthy heart, you probably would have covered exercise, nutrition, and even attitude. So, you could send your query "10 Great Exercises for a Healthy Heart" to your favorite health and fitness magazine. You could send your query "10 Tasty Foods That Guard Your Heart's Health" to a nutrition-oriented health magazine. You could try your query "Loving Attitudes for a Longer Life" to your favorite health magazine that, likewise, appreciates the view that emotions play a decided role in heart health. Remember to use titles, though, that are in keeping with the style and length of the titles used in your target magazine.

When you are judicious regarding the publishers with whom you deal, you can enjoy the luxury of presenting your queries to multiple publications at the same time. In the case of publishers who purchase one-time print rights, simultaneous print rights, and electronic rights, and who like to see completed work, you have the option to submit your typescripts to several noncompeting publications at once. In the case of publishers who run reprints, you have the opportunity and pleasure to resell your work because you wisely retained your rights. The key is to be prudent with the placement of your work and to know your markets well on local, regional, national, and international levels.

If you are publishing your polished work consistently in national publications and wish to expand your horizons into international markets, be sure to acquaint yourself with *Writers News* and *Writing Magazine* (P.O. Box 4, Nairn, Scotland IV12 4HU). These companion resources include guidance from top writing professionals around the world, interviews, reviews, and more; and they introduce a treasure chest of international markets. Remember to order sample copies of the publications of interest to you as well as their contributor's guidelines so that you can proceed in a professional manner that the international editors will appreciate.

Paying Attention to Cultures and Customs

If you are interested in international publications, also acquaint yourself with *Ulrich's International Periodicals Directory*. Acquire and study sample copies of any publications of interest to you. Always compose your article specifically for its country. Stay alert for topics that can have universal appeal.

Know cultural differences, religious differences, and social mores, and respect and honor those differences. Certainly, you will want to match your topic, tone, style, language, and cultural preferences to any of your international submissions. Also, include interviews with experts or celebrities that fit the varying levels, different countries, and interesting cultures. If you are writing an article for a New York publication, it is a good idea to include information from New York experts. Some of the same quoted materials might serve your article for Australia, also, but include information from Australian experts, too. When you submit articles to publications that use British spelling, do yourself a favor and submit your work using British spelling.

In addition to traveling and learning from experience about cultures and customs different from your own, reading and researching to be knowledgeable also can serve you well. You also may rely on international friends. I have writer friends in Australia, Bangladesh, and India who can give a quick read to my typescripts that would serve those audiences, respectively. They can read with attention to details to help make sure that my words are perfectly suited to the intended audience, that terms are used with clarity, and that my sentiment would not be offensive. I, in turn, do such a favor for international writer friends who choose to write for American publications and want a final check on the articles before submitting them.

Take time to explore each of your target publications. Ask yourself questions you may not have asked yourself ever before as a "reader" of the magazine.

- Do all the articles in your target magazine nab the reader's attention and thrust toward a single big picture?
- Do the articles supply a potpourri of ideas?
- Can you determine the mission of your target market?

Production Editor Donna Welsh of North Sydney, NSW, Australia, shares that the mission of *WellBeing* magazine is both personal and planetary healing. *WellBeing* "maintains a loyal readership because of its up-to-the-minute and practical, promotion-free information that is easy for its readers to implement."

- Does your target publication pride itself on testing the products that it advertises and attempting to review those products without bias?

Judi Becker of Austin, Texas, believes the integrity of *Good Dog!* and *CATsumer Report* keeps her readers coming back again and again. She says, "When we review a product, for instance, we do it with no bias. We try to make certain that our facts are straight concerning the product we've tested and reviewed. If we have any questions or doubts, we call the manufacturer. We think our readers like this—our integrity."

Go on to ask yourself these questions.

- Can you determine the goal of your target magazine?
- Is your target publication service-oriented?
- Does your target publication primarily educate or primarily entertain?
- Do your own personal attitudes coincide with the values of your target publication?
- Are you on the same wavelength with your target publication?

One way to test yourself is to note whether or not you are a user of the products the magazine advertises.

- Do special theme issues come out seasonally or annually?
- Do the topics cluster around people, animals, places, products, or qualities?
- Does every issue feature a famous person or teach about a rare bird or warn of political crisis?
- Does every issue give information about caring for your exotic automobile?
- Does every issue give information about new FDA rulings?
- Does every issue whisk you to a honeymoon hideaway or pioneer a colorful new product?
- Does every issue scrutinize qualities like love, fear, anger, or jealousy?
- Do the titles take the same structural form throughout the magazine?
- Are all the titles brief?

- Are titles and subtitles used?
- Are the titles given in the form of a question?
- Do the titles startle the reader?

Think through all these questions and others of your own as you decide your topic. Give your topic a slant that you know—from your familiarity with the publication—will be of keen interest to the editor. Write down some possible topics. Do any of your topics touch numerous bases of interest—finances, health, children, pets, or inventions? Quickly, think of some topics that you have wished to read about or topics that would be natural followups for existing articles. Instantly, you may have a winning idea for a super article and be on the right track. Welcome aboard!

• • •

Chapter 3. Finding Your Dream Publications

You are enchanted with a glossy magazine. You compose queries for it in your mind as you shower and dress then fight the traffic on the way to your office. You repeat your ideas. You memorize your thoughts to freeze them in place. You fret that in the heat of the day your thoughts will melt then evaporate before you have your chance to write them down. You can hardly wait to prepare your query. Constant intrusions keep you from your goal. You feel anxious. You must write your query and submit it. When will you ever have the time?

Wait. How well do you know your dream market? Even in this age of social informality, proper introductions to publications are a must for writers. Always get acquainted with your potential magazines before you fall for them. Some publications may have lovely faces but cold hearts.

Learning about Your Dream Market

Always go straight to your current annual *Writer's Market* and to your up-to-the-minute market reports such as Angela Adair-Hoy's *The Write Markets Report*, Kathryn Ptacek's *Gila Queen's Guide to Markets, The Writer, Writer's Digest, Writers News,* and *Writing Magazine*. Read any sections that report problems with publications. Make sure that your dream magazine has good marks. Especially if several writers reveal unfortunate dealings with a particular publication, it may be prudent to steer clear. Look for another magazine that covers the same type of material that you write. If your favorite magazine has received high marks for its dealings with writers, and their writer's guidelines are available at your local writer's league or writer's club, dash there and read them; or order their guidelines promptly. If the market guides do not reveal much about how your target magazine treats writers, consult your writer friends. Here are a fistful of questions you might like to ask.

Learning from Your Writer Friends

- Have your writer friends written for your dream market?
- Did your dream magazine permit simultaneous queries or simultaneous submissions of typescripts?

- Did your writer friends receive a fair contract with terms spelled out clearly?
- Was the contract sent promptly?
- How did their assignments go?
- How well did their communications with the editor go?
- How soon did they learn of their acceptance?
- Were they promised payment on acceptance?
- Were they to be paid upon publication?
- Were the editor's instructions clear?
- Were they asked to do rewrites? If so, was the editor helpful and clear with instructions?
- Did the editor call for an entirely new piece because of a change in his plans? If so, did he increase their compensation?
- If the editor rewrote any large portions of their work, did the editor ask their approval and give them the opportunity to withdraw the story?
- Did the editor want any local or regional acquaintances, political, or social figures stuffed into the article or touted?
- Did the editor want advertisers plugged?
- How soon were their pieces published?
- Were their works published with care?
- Did the editorial staff butcher the names of any of their experts or leave out the experts' affiliation, thus causing problems for your writer friends with that noteworthy person?
- When the editor was asked to print a correction, did he follow through with a correction? Or did he ignore your writer friends and leave them to deal with the expert's hurt feelings?
- Were they pleased with illustrations that the editor added?
- Did the illustrations accurately complement their text?
- Did the writers supply illustrations or photographs?
- What rights to their transparencies or photographs were purchased?
- Did they receive extra compensation for their photography?
- Were photographs required as part of the assignment, but without additional compensation for the photos?
- Were they given a byline for their photographs?

- How much were they paid for their articles?
- How promptly did their checks arrive?
- Have your writer friends built a long-standing relationship with the editor?
- Do they feel a loyalty to the editor and wish to continue the special writer-editor partnership?

Regarding payment, think of it this way—had your writer friend gone on a long holiday to Costa Rica and his electricity bill arrived the day after his departure, he could have returned to a dark house and a fine for his overdue payment. Writers provide a service just as an electric department provides a service; therefore, writers also deserve to be paid.

So prepare to sell your work many times. Many publishers buy reprint rights and are pleased to share useful "perennial" articles with their readers. Many times, you can update the work to be reprinted and add bonus materials. The publishers benefit, the readers benefit, and so do you. Resales help to pay for your overhead, office furniture, computer, printer and laser cartridges, bond paper, and photocopy machine, not to mention your health insurance. Because you bear these expenses rather than the editorial offices for whom you work, you are a welcome long-distance "team" player.

Knowing Your Rights to Sell

If your dream publication typically Buys All Rights, you may decide to avoid it rather than to accept that single check and give up the lucrative opportunities to earn numerous checks from your hard-researched information and hard-earned interview materials.

When a publisher, who buys all rights, reprints your article or story, you will not receive an additional payment. The publisher owns the work. The publisher may choose to reprint your work many times. Some publishers who buy all rights do not even give you a byline.

You also will want to avoid contracts that force you to work for hire. With those, too, you most often would receive no byline. In addition, you have no rights to your materials after publication. You should have the right to sell your hard-researched work to other publishers. To be fair to yourself, you may decide to deal only with publishers who purchase First Print Serial Rights, One-time Print Rights, Simultaneous Print Rights, or Reprint Rights, to mention a few of the more desirable sales possibilities.

Recognizing your expenditure of time makes it clear why you should refuse to sell all rights. Think about your efforts to collect information, arrange and conduct interviews, then sort and assimilate the information to compose, revise, and polish your article. Add the price for your internet service, special library expenses, and travel, and you have incurred abundant expenses, all for the love of writing. If your goal is to earn from your hard work, retaining rights to your materials makes good sense.

Supporting the Writing Profession

When you refuse to sign contracts that force you to sell all rights or force you to work for hire, you help to support the writing profession and to elevate the working conditions for all writers. If all writers would refuse such contracts, perhaps such contracts would cease to exist.

According to the American Society of Journalists and Authors Code of Ethics and Fair Practices, which is printed annually in the ASJA Directory, "It shall be understood, unless otherwise stipulated in writing, that sale of an article manuscript entitles the purchaser to first North American publication rights only, and that all other rights are retained by the author. Under no circumstances shall an independent writer be required to sign a so-called 'all rights transferred' or 'work made for hire' agreement as a condition of assignment, of payment, or of publication."

Learning from the American Society of Journalists and Authors (ASJA)

In addition, keep in mind the prudent advice of ASJA "Contract tips: Electronic rights in newspaper and magazine contracts" that "All uses beyond first print publication must be separately licensed and separately compensated." Likewise, writers should be cognizant of ASJA's sober guidance that "It is not acceptable to take a higher overall fee to surrender electronic rights with print rights." So, be sure to get a separate electronic rights agreement for which you will be paid. Sell electronic rights for a clearly designated period of time, not for perpetual electronic reuse.

Recently, an online publisher sent me a contract which proposed the purchase of all rights. I amended the contract to "First Online Rights Only," which I defined to mean that the particular publisher would have the license for "First Internet Use" for a period of up to four years from the date of publication, not for perpetual electronic reuse. As the author, I would retain all other Electronic Rights such as the rights to sell and distribute the work on CD ROM, to store the work in a database, such as Lexis-Nexus, and to sell the articles to electronic media not yet invented. As the author, I also would retain all print and all other media rights. I also added that if he would wish to publish my articles in a print publication, we could negotiate a price for either first North American print serial rights, one-time rights, simultaneous rights, or reprint rights. He accepted my amendments, and we proceeded.

Remember that you can delete from contracts clauses that force you to "sell rights to all versions of the work by all means whether 'now known or hereafter created, invented, or developed' in perpetuity throughout the world," or you simply can refuse to sign if the publisher will not negotiate equitably.

In "Contract Tips: Watch out for these clauses," ASJA also emphasizes the necessity of revising proposed contracts to read as "First North American PRINT serial rights," and they advise adding the explanatory clause, "All rights not expressly transferred herein are reserved by the author." ASJA empowers writers with indispensable information on magazine and newspaper publishers to help them negotiate out of a base of knowledge and strength.

Learning about Contracts

The ASJA website includes a full, searchable archive of past editions of Contracts Watch as well as tips on freelance contracts, electronic rights, and copyright. You can receive each issue of ASJA Contracts Watch by e-mail automatically at no charge.

Contracts, of course, vary from publisher to publisher. Basic contracts will state the title of your work and its expected word length, the rights being purchased, the amount of your payment and when it will be posted—on acceptance or on publication. The contract also will bear a statement that you guarantee your work to be original and accurate, to the best of your knowledge. It also will state that all-important deadline that you must honor. Some contracts also offer a kill fee which pays you some portion of the original agreed-upon amount if your work is good but the editor cannot publish it for some reason.

Knowing the Purpose of Contracts

Contracts should protect both the writer and the publisher. Some contracts, though, hold writers responsible against any litigious actions brought about from their materials perceived to libel or to defame. You will not want to sign any contract that places you in such a position.

The American Society of Journalists and Authors Code of Ethics and Fair Practices states this best—"No writer should be obliged to indemnify any magazine or book publisher against any claim, actions, or proceedings arising from an article or book."

Preparing a Letter of Confirmation

If you query a publisher and the editor phones to assign you the work, listen to his instructions and take careful notes. Especially after spoken instructions, if a contract will not be sent, or for any assignment that does not include a contract, you may wish to write a letter of confirmation. Describe your assignment as you understand it. Be sure to include your working title, a brief outline of your plan to achieve your goal, the length expected, the rights sold to the publisher, the payment to be received for the text upon acceptance or upon publication, the payment to be received for any photographs or transparencies, and your agreed-upon deadline. Be certain to enumerate his instructions as clearly and succinctly as you can, and post your confirmation letter to the editor. Such a letter can be helpful to clarify your understanding of your obligation to the editor. Be sure to enclose your SASE. The editor can help to clarify further any terms that he may wish to address, or your confirmation letter can stand as presented to bind your agreement.

There are many wonderful editors and publishers to whom you can submit your queries, and upon receiving a go-ahead, you later can submit your carefully researched and prepared articles. ASJA can speed your search for the finest publishers.

Choosing Your Publications with Care

You may decide not to deal with any publications that respond only if interested. How long would you wait on those? Don't torture yourself. You deserve to receive a reply rather than to be kept wondering.

Waiting for a Response

You should not have to wait for an unreasonably long time for one publisher to decide on your query or proposal. Neither should you have to wait such an extended period to see your accepted typescript in print. If a publisher holds a typescript for six months without adding it to his publication lineup or holds work for a year without publishing it, "all rights therein should revert to the author without penalty or cost to the author," according to the American Society of Journalists and Authors Code of Ethics and Fair Practices.

If the editor does hold your work for a long period of time so that you must update your information before its final delayed publication, you can ask for an increase in the payment to compensate for your additional work.

Sometimes, though, there are unavoidable delays that turn out to be pleasant surprises, if you can be patient. David P. Robson, former Editor of *Chem Matters*, an award-winning magazine for educational journalism, held an article of mine to run it as a cover story. My complimentary copy and check arrived with a note that said, "Thank you again for your effort on this project ["Contact Lenses"]. We are sorry about the delay, but I think it was worth the wait. It's a great cover story."

Knowing Your Submission Rights

If your target magazine does not permit simultaneous queries and simultaneous submissions, you may choose to look for a different one. It is to your benefit to deal with publishers who permit simultaneous queries or typescripts. If you do submit queries or typescripts to editors who request being informed of simultaneous submissions, either honor their wishes or prepare queries with very different slants so that if both editors accept your proposal, you can make both happy.

You can consider paying publications only, as well, if you choose. On the other hand, if you love writing and sharing information, you may enjoy preparing work for the joy of seeing it published and to earn your first clips. It is all up to you.

Wendy McCallum, Co-Editor of *Healthy Options*, Tauranga, New Zealand, says, "Even if the financial return for an accepted article may not compensate the initial time and effort put in, I suggest making that extra effort to impress the editor and get your writer's foot in the door."

Even after you do "get your foot in the door," it pays to care about your work, to be punctual, and to be cordial to your editor. Recently, when I received a note from Jan Werblin, Associate Editor of *Professional Counselor Magazine,* to confirm the arrival of my first print rights assignment, she said:

Linda,

Thanks for once again going that extra mile. I have had a chance to scan your article, but I haven't yet read through it. It looks great, though—chock full of useful info and credible sources. Good job.

Jan

To get an idea of the competition you are up against, check the listing of your target in the *Writer's Market* for the number of submissions received by the publisher annually. In addition, check to see how soon your submission will be published, if accepted. If your material is timely, most editors will not let it languish. Keep in mind, though, that many editors have a lead time of from three to 12 months. So place your hot items carefully so they will be published before they cool off.

Pitching Only Well-Targeted Queries

Anthony Mark Dalessandro, former Editor of *Italian America*, Washington, D.C., says, "Many writers do not seem to learn much about the magazines that they send submissions to. Seems like a lot of writers simply learn what the title is and assume too much. I get a lot of submissions that aren't even close to anything we would consider running."

Similarly, Debbie Ridpath Ohi, whom you met in Chapter 2, says, "Read the writer's guidelines before submitting a query or an article. Read back issues of the magazine. This advice seems obvious, but many beginning writers seem to ignore it. I get fiction pieces submitted to *Inklings* all the time, for example, even though I don't publish fiction."

Editors are confronted daily with queries and submissions that are not remotely related to the heart or soul of their publications. Editors are weary of this time-consuming problem. It wastes editors' time, and it wastes writers' time.

Carol Schaal, the Managing Editor of *Notre Dame Magazine*, Notre Dame, Indiana, also says she finds that too many writers do not follow even the basic suggestions of studying sample copies and writer's guidelines of target magazines to match topic, tone, and style. She says, "The staff enjoys working with freelancers; but all too frequently we receive queries and transom pieces that simply have no relevance to our publication."

Reading thought-provoking articles such as "Possession Obsession and the Right Stuff," by the managing editor, "The Thing Is" by Editor Kerry Temple, "The Meaning of Things" by Associate Editor John Monczunski, and "For What It's Worth" by Associate Editor Ed Cohen can help you to recognize the kind of articles they would consider. You must read and study many articles from many issues, though, before submitting a query—your sales pitch to your target editor. Querying saves time for both you and your editor, and it allows her to guide you regarding her goals for her magazine.

As you read and study your target magazine think about what draws you to it.

- Are you clear about the scope and tone of the magazine?
- Why does this magazine have loyal readers?

Gena Holle, Editor of *The International Railway Traveler* in San Diego, says that her readers keep coming back because besides mainstream rail coverage—Amtrak, France's TGVs, luxury trains—IRT "offers stories you won't find in other rail magazines, off-the-beaten-track destinations that open new possibilities for the intrepid rail traveler who is looking for a unique rail adventure. And, armchair travelers take delight in vicarious journeys to exotic lands, from Cuba to Fiji to Namibia, to name a few."

- What intrigues you as a reader? If you can flip through the magazine without ever being captured by an intriguing title or topic, other readers may also.
- Can you hardly put away the magazine once you begin reading? Why? What mesmerizes you?

- Do you read article after article eagerly?

It is prudent to submit your query only if you can you see your work fitting between two existing articles in your target magazine and you can see your article supporting the expected level and quality of information of the magazine.

- Can you see your service article building on the information shared in this month's service article?
- Can you write an article that you feel could replace an article in your target magazine?

Interpreting Your Findings

When you have landed a topic, pared it, molded it, and slanted it, check the magazine's most current index, if it has one. If you find nothing on your topic, search deeper into past issues. If you can go back two to three years in most magazines without finding an article that has been published on your topic, it can mean that the magazine editor is not interested in such a topic, even though you thought she could be.

On the contrary, it could mean that it is just about time for an article on the angle of your topic. Continue to check similar topics. Is your subject taboo with your editor? Has your subject merely been neglected? Peruse the *Reader's Guide to Periodical Literature* to see if your unique idea has been reported already in your target magazine. If it has not and you believe that you have a good lead and that you can produce an article and even peg it for a seasonal event, then prepare your query.

Exploring More Specific Target Magazines

Study the last 12 to 24 issues of your target magazine or newspaper.

- Are the pieces in the form of interviews, or are they merely straight narrative?
- Does each issue have a theme?
- Are queries required, or does the editor prefer that completed typescripts be submitted?
- Can you supply a needed story?
- If your target journal or magazine documents materials, which style sheet is followed?
- Study the photographs. Does the editor require that photos accompany your article?

- Does the editor want color transparencies or black and white photos?
- Can you supply color transparencies with excellent composition to give your sports story an edge?
- Can you supply black and white photographs to support your story?

If you wish to be published in a literary journal, then read and study an ample number of issues to get a feel for the writing styles the editors appreciate and the themes they embrace.

- Are the titles long or short?
- Are the titles posed as questions?
- Are titles and subtitles used?
- Are headings and subheadings used in the body of the text of every article or story?
- Can you write on a suitable topic for the magazine?
- Does your genre and style fit the magazine?

If you have an idea for an article that will fit under the journal's umbrella, then send your carefully prepared query. When you receive the go-ahead, make your work compatible with the other articles and stories in the journal.

Reading the Newspaper, Magazine, or Journal Completely

Wherever your interest lies, inform yourself fully about that market. Sara Gilbert, Editor, *U.S. Art*, Minneapolis, Minnesota, comments, "My biggest beef is with writers who insist that their story is right for our magazine when they obviously have never read it."

Don't just read an article or two. Read the newspaper, magazine, or journal completely. Read and analyze the masthead. Compare the staff names with the bylines given. What percentage of articles are produced by freelance writers? What will be your chance to have your query secure an assignment? Your chance may be minuscule if the newspaper or magazine of your choice buys only one or two freelance articles a month. Still, you can give it a try.

Guy Lancaster, Editorial Assistant of *The Arkansas Review: A Journal of Delta Studies* in Jonesboro, Arkanas, agrees completely with Gilbert. Give sober consideration to his helpful commentary.

Know your market. Our magazine publishes articles, stories, poems, interviews, photographs, and art that evoke the seven states, from Illinois down to Louisiana, that make up the Mississippi River Delta. However, we regularly receive submissions that do not fall within this editorial focus. One person sent a story about living in Saudi Arabia, and another person submitted a story about skiing in the Rockies. We also do not accept simultaneous submissions, but we receive them daily. When we get submissions like this, we know they are from people who know the mailing address of our journal and nothing else. Anyone looking to be published in our magazine will find it immensely beneficial to buy a sample issue or subscribe or, at the least, to look at our website, where we have submission guidelines posted. Any regular reader of our magazine knows that we are always looking for pieces that have something new to say about the Delta region, not pieces coated in cliché regionalisms. Our magazine may be devoted to one specific region, but it is going to take more than country folk speaking in Mark Twain dialogues to make a story acceptable for us. There are many unheard voices in the Delta, and we want to hear them. The Delta is another setting for the human drama.

Paying close attention to the combined advice of all the editors who have been kind enough to share their comments in *The Writer's Friend* can help to make you more calamity-resistant when it comes to dealing with editors. Some may even want you to join their team. Many cordial editors are waiting for your carefully targeted queries and typescripts. You can find them, if you try.

Evaluating Your Chances for Sales

To boost your chances for sales, you also may choose to look for a publication that appeals to you that receives a relatively small number of submissions each year. If you receive a "go-ahead," that's great. If not, analyze your query and revise it for greater clarity, if needed. Study the next publication of interest to you and submit your new query molded precisely to fit that market.

Above all, make sure that the topic, angle, and depth will suit your potential market. Try to match your talent with the target magazine of your choice and keep pitching carefully crafted queries until you meet your goal. Never give up. Find your dream market, and contribute to it. Happy marketing!

• • •

Chapter 4.
Knowing Your Audience

Tim Horan, the Managing Editor of *The Greyhound Review*, Abilene, Kansas, says that if freelance writers would just do their homework, then they would find it much easier to sell their work. They should follow writer's guidelines and also show that they have studied their target publication and contemplated the audience that the magazine's advertising targets. They should pitch a winning topic (with a good hook) appropriate to the magazine. They should have credentials or the ability to supply fine research and excellent interviews. In addition, it is useful if they can offer good quality photos. He says that most writers don't understand his audience and emphasizes that "It doesn't matter how good the writing is if it doesn't fit the audience."

As you study your target publications, be sure to pay attention to their locations and to their advertisers to recognize obvious topics of interest and to glean subtle nuances that reveal the heart of the magazine.

Notice the wide range of topics of some magazines and the laser-beam focus of others. Some publications have worldwide general audiences. Some publications may be devoted entirely to the politics, culture, and fashion of a single nation. Some may blend fascinating interlinkings of different countries and cultures. Still others may focus on a single city and its citizens. Some may be dedicated to serving one group or club within a single city or be devoted to one sport or one activity. As you begin to read more and more from the viewpoint of a writer, you will be able to analyze each publication easily and quickly.

Reading and Studying Your Target Publication

Canada—

Jim Adair, whom you met in Chapter 2 "Getting on the Right Track," Editor-in-Chief of *Homes & Cottages*, says, "Keep regional differences in mind. We are a Canadian magazine, yet we constantly get stories with U.S.-only themes."

Adair does not mean that themes that blend Canadian and U.S. themes are not considered, however. "A Taste of Mexico" by Elsie Rose that ran in *Homes & Cottages* introduced a grand home—the art work of architect Roman M. Kujath, an Edmonton, Alberta architect—nestled on the spectacular shores of Skaha Lake in the Okanagan Valley not far from Penticton, British Columbia. Just as Kujath, the architect, says, "This house is very aesthetically pleasing, and it fits well into the environment," this article about a Canadian couple's dream home of modern Mexican design fits well in *Homes & Cottages* magazine. Guests even say they can see Zorro living there.

South Africa—

Vanessa Raphaely, Editor of *Cosmopolitan*, Cape Town, South Africa, reminds writers that "One of the most important tips when writing for an edition of an international brand is to study *THAT* edition, not to assume that, for example, because you are familiar with an American edition you will instantly understand the South African one. It's that new cliché: Think local; act global."

United States—

Regarding paying attention to location, Lisa Rosenthal, Editor of *San Francisco Peninsula Parent*, says that she is always looking for a local angle on subjects relating to parenting because her publication is a "local" parenting publication. She says that *SFPP* is the only source of local information for parents and that her local connections and local calendar keep her readers coming back again and again.

Articles such as Rose Heller's "San Francisco Superintendent Bill Rojas Speaks Out" are of interest to her local readers.

Spain—

G.W. Amick, Editor of *The First Word Bulletin*, Madrid, Spain, laments that writers do not pay attention to his location in still another way. "I am in Spain but receive SASEs with American stamps on the envelope which I can't use."

Adair of *Homes & Cottages* can empathize with Amick's SASE problem. Adair says, "We also get lots of self-addressed, stamped reply envelopes with U.S. postage. U.S. postage doesn't work here." These editors appreciate receiving international reply coupons (IRCs) with submissions.

So, in addition to paying attention to location, what are some other ways to help pinpoint your audience?

Identifying Your Audience

Raphaely of *Cosmopolitan* recommends "respect for the reader as a good kick-off." She says to "figure out who the magazine is aimed at and address *them*."

Check the pulse of your target publication. Write down your impressions of the magazine's cover and its articles.

- Does the cover catch your eye? If so, why?

- Can you recognize issue after issue as that particular publication just by its cover?
- What makes that publication unique?

To learn about your audience, study the feature articles very closely. Ask yourself the following questions.

- What intrigues the readers?
- What keeps them buying the magazine?
- Are the readers loyal for many years, or do they outgrow their need for the magazine?
- Are the articles features, essays, or reports?
- Are they service oriented?
- Do the articles educate?
- What level of expertise must the reader already have about the topic to understand the articles presented?
- Do the articles and stories entertain?
- Are the articles photo-driven?
- Are the illustrations or photos so excellent they almost tell the story without text?
- What is the publication's mission?
- Do the articles presented in the magazine seem to have only one voice?
- Can you detect numerous individual writer's voices?
- What concerns do the readers have?

For several days think about what you have discovered. Then study all of those issues again. Write down your impressions of the covers and the articles.

- Have your impressions changed?
- What insights do you feel you now have that you did not have upon your first study?

Close attention to the details and approaches of the articles will help you to answer all these questions and paint a portrait of your readers.

Reading Letters from Readers

If you read the Letters from Readers section or the Letters to the Editor section of the magazine, you may get an even more vivid image of your target reader.

- What concerns do the readers have?
- If you are studying the letters from readers of a parenting magazine, do some readers need support if they choose to stay home to love and care for their tykes?
- On the opposite side, do other readers need support if they choose to find a loving caregiver and return to work?

Parents and parents-to-be often are concerned with the health and safety of their youngsters. Are they also interested in housing, toys, entertainment, play groups, travel, and finances as these relate to their tots? Their letters reveal a treasure trove of potential articles.

Reading Notes from the Editor

Certainly, always read letters or notes from the editor. Read and study their articles that are included in your target magazine, as well. Their letters or notes and articles will give you insight into the their thoughts, values, goals, and sense of humor.

Read these pieces from many issues to find the passion of the editor of your target magazine. If you and your potential editor have similar philosophies and similar passions, you may be just the writer that particular editor has hoped to find.

To write well for a magazine, it is important that you have a genuine appreciation for the publication. If you do not like to read the magazine, you will not like to write for it.

Paying Attention to the Advertising Focus

Examine six or eight of the most recent issues of your target publication and analyze the advertisements to determine a profile of the readers.

Do the ads speak to you? If your target magazine is your favorite magazine, ask yourself why it is and what keeps you reading it year after year. What do you believe you have in common with the other readers of this magazine? Think about it. You probably do not read magazines whose ads offend you.

Advertisers spend countless thousands of dollars to recognize their audiences. Studying and dissecting the magazine advertisements places crucial information at your fingertips. Your analysis will uncover a treasure map to the sale of your article. You will realize the slant or focus that will appeal to the editor and the readers. You may even let the advertising blaze the trail to help you come up with a catchy "working" title for your topic of interest. Staking out a territory to explore will help you zero in to compose a power-packed article. You will keep out extraneous material.

Like it or not, in many cases you must keep your articles compatible with the bent of the sponsors of your target magazines. While some editors do not allow advertising and editorial copy to entwine themselves as bedfellows, the cold, hard fact is that you probably will not sell an article on "The Hazards of Smoking" to magazines whose sponsors include cigarette companies. But, then, anything is possible, so perhaps it could happen.

The ads are so scarce and so subtly placed in some magazines that, to the casual reader, the tastes of the audience may not be obvious, at first. The ads in other magazines are so abundant you may have difficulty navigating through to locate the articles.

Analyzing Ads to Reveal Readers

Magazines landscaped with colorful, full-page ads that practically shout about the lifestyles, intellects, and attitudes of their readers can be quite revealing as you analyze them.

Notice the ages, images, clothing styles, and appeal of the people depicted in the ads to provide the clues you need. Do the ads appeal to a budget-oriented audience or an audience of affluent readers? Is the magazine stuffed with dollars-off coupons, or do the ads lure readers to travel to exotic destinations?

• An Affluent Audience

If the glossy double-page ad displays an exquisite diamond and emerald bracelet, the wealthy reader whom you visualize, quite accurately, may be lounging on the deck of a yacht sipping a martini. The magazine, doubtless, addresses a wealthy readership. The readers might enjoy articles on "Midnight Mediterranean Cruises" or "10 Sizzling Spas."

• A Cost-Conscious Audience

If the half-page ad shows Carter's Baby Basics or Just One Year or Carter's Classics, it is possible that the rushed reader, attuned to the essentials, is about to drop off the youngster of the house at kindergarten, give the tyke a big hug, then dash to a bustling downtown office to work from nine to five. This reader would likely welcome hints on "Ways to Put More Hours in the Day."

Would this reader be interested in the latest word on safe herbal remedies for toddlers? Are the ads for pharmaceuticals or herbs? If there are ads for pharmaceuticals, probably an article on herbal remedies would not be welcome.

If fathers are depicted readily in the advertisements of magazines for expectant and new parents, articles oriented to speak to new fathers also may be welcome. Some magazines focus on the mother more fully, yet address the needs and questions of new fathers, too. Some address the needs of fathers first and foremost, yet also share caring information for both father and mother. If you pay close attention, you will know precisely how to focus your article.

Do any ads depict the single parent—female or male? Does the magazine address the issue of single parenting?

With careful slanting, you conceivably can supply noncompeting publications with crucial information. You can address the needs of a variety of parenting possibilities.

Analyzing Mail Order Classifieds

Don't overlook the tiny mail order classifieds in the backs of some magazines. These, too, help you to visualize your typical readers so that you can come up with topics of interest to them.   Keen attention to advertising slant can help you to target sale after sale effectively.

As mentioned in Chapter 2, "Getting on the Right Track," you shop with discriminating taste, you dine in your favorite restaurants, and you choose your companions with care. Shopping wisely for the right magazine for your unique ideas will work for you, too, and your earnings will increase dramatically and promptly.

Perusing Specialty Magazines

Magazines for Brides

Some audiences are quite obvious by their titles. Still you must study the content of several issues to find clues that will make your queries winners. Sometimes you can produce good followup articles with an opposite slant from a current article on the newsstand, if the topic is not already in queue. If a bridal magazine presents a "Going All Out" article about weddings, the editor also may be looking for an article about "Simplifying Weddings in a

Busy World." As a followup to either of these approaches, you might query with "Making Your Guests Feel Welcome," for whether an elaborate or a modest ceremony, one of the beautiful aspects of a wedding is to share joy with the families and friends of the happy couple. Making the guests feel welcome is the ideal way to accomplish this goal.

The Quarter Horse Journal

Also, as you study magazines, pay close attention to their affiliations. If you are preparing a piece for *The Quarter Horse Journal*, founded in 1948 by Raymond Hollingworth, you will note its affiliation with the American Quarter Horse Association. You also will see that it keeps its readers updated on "activities of the Quarter Horse on the range, in the arena, in the show ring, and on the short track." In addition, you will recognize that the journal has knowledgeable readers, many of whom have been loyal readers for more than 40 years.

The ads of *The Quarter Horse Journal* sell not only horses but also everything from automatic insect control systems to trailers. Now you know that you can pitch an article on "Quarter horse show ring tips," or you might cover the next AQHA Youth World Cup.

In this particular case, the title of the magazine proudly presents the topic and related topics that will appeal to its readers. Still you must study the magazine to know precisely how to focus your queries and articles to meet the requirements and desires of the editor.

In addition, the ads profile the tastes of your audience. Diligent study of the ads can lead you to unlimited possibilities for perfectly targeted topics to pitch to editors.

Inflight Magazines

If you are interested in writing for inflight magazines, it is important to know the geographic areas they serve. Read widely to get a good overall idea about those different locations. Also find out what types of general interest articles the editor runs. What picturesque location do they serve but have not profiled for a year or more? Can you support your article with striking photos or transparencies?

Finding Out about a More Elusive Audience

If the magazine that you are about to query contains no advertisements, then you will need to read not only the mission statement, if the magazine shares one, but also you will want to study several back issues to analyze the titles, the prominent themes, and the direction of the publication. If the magazine has won any awards, you will want to note the group that bestowed the honors. Even that can help to delineate the reading audience. Such a quiet magazine's needs may be obvious so that it proves to be an easy publication to approach with queries, as well, especially if you read and study it with attention to its editorial slant.

If you study the articles and the ads, you may come to believe the Chinese proverb, "One picture is worth a thousand words," for the illustrations that complement magazine ads definitely will help you to determine which thousand words your audience is eager to read.

Finding Out about Release Forms

If you are wondering about inserting such items as names of businesses, entertainment places, or airlines in your articles and wonder if you need the permission from them, it is best to find out what your target publication requires.

Requirements vary from editor to editor. Chad Schlegel, Managing Editor of *Lakeland Boating* magazine, *Great Lakes Angler* magazine, and *Ports O' Call Cruising Guides,* says, "Our attitude is that if a company is in business, it's fair game. We sometimes run into problems when local merchants get angry because a writer focused on one shop or restaurant and overlooked others. We figure it's important to be as thorough as possible and mention as many businesses by name as space allows; favorites just get a little more ink."

Joanne Cosker, the Assistant Editor of *The Educated Traveler,* Chantilly, Virginia, says, "Since the majority of our articles deal primarily with pointing readers to special interest tour operators, places or events, our writers do not need permission from these businesses to use their names. In fact, we receive many calls from businesses begging us to write about them!"

From a quite different viewpoint, you will find according to *The Write Markets Report,* February 1998 issue, p. 11, that *Mobility,* a "magazine that addresses all topics relating to the moving industry and corporate relocation assistance," says: "Regardless of your topic, articles accepted for publication must be previously unpublished and contain no commercial message."

Being Aware of Diametrically Opposed Views

You will note that two of these editors have very similar criteria while the third is at the opposite end of the spectrum regarding using names of businesses, entertainment places, and airlines. Because requirements can be so different, the necessity of studying guidelines and sample copies of your target publications is of utmost importance. What is right for one editor is material for rejection for another editor. You cannot overfamiliarize yourself with what your target magazine requires and appreciates. Find out what each editor wants. Then precisely supply those needs. It works.

Targeting Technical Writing

Regarding the importance of defining your purpose and targeting your audience in technical writing, Gregg says, "Before you write a single word, you need to know who will read what you are writing. By analyzing your audience, you know how much information to present and how to present it. You will present less technical information to high school biology students than to research scientists. You don't want to go over the users' heads; they'll get frustrated. You don't want to go below their level of knowledge; they'll be either bored or insulted. Your document also needs a purpose, so you don't throw extraneous information into the document or leave out important information."Gregg's words apply equally to nonfiction for popular magazines.

Targeting Fiction Writing

If you are a fiction writer, it is equally important to study your markets. Editor and Publisher Anne Kennedy says, "I publish work that is too bizarre for mainstream, yet it doesn't fit the standard mold of science fiction, fantasy, or horror. The work I publish cannot be easily classified. Some may be disturbed by something that has no label, but my readers love it!"

She goes on to say, "Professional writers bring with them their names, which can draw a larger audience to any publication. I do not publish work by "name" authors simply to put their names on the cover. The work must earn its place in my magazine. I've turned down many stories written by professional writers because those stories didn't fit the tone of *The Silver Web*. This makes it a bit different from other magazines. Maybe the degree of difficulty in getting published in it is a challenge to some writers. I receive approximately 50 manuscripts every day, yet I only publish 10-16 a year, so you can see that *The Silver Web* is a tough market to crack."

Once again, you see the significance of studying each market to understand its very essence.

• • •

I appreciate authors who make the effort to spell my name correctly and who send their queries to the right e-mail address.

Debbie Ridpath Ohi
INKLINGS
Toronto, Ontario
Canada

Many times I can just look at the envelope and form an opinion. When I open the envelope, my opinion is justified. Just as I thought, no cover letter. You already know which basket that envelope went in. Yes, I like it; or no, I don't. The envelope, the paper, the presentation, the first paragraph must grab my attention. Of course the body of the story sells the story, not the first paragraph....

G.W. Amick
FIRST WORD BULLETIN
Madrid, Spain

Freelancers hate getting rejection form letters from editors, but guess what? Editors hate getting form letters from freelancers who are obviously pitching the same idea to dozens of publications, without regard to regional differences or to what the magazine covers.

Jim Adair
HOMES & GARDENS
Mississauga, Ontario
Canada

It needs to be obvious that writers have studied my publication and our guidelines by adhering to the suggestions in the guidelines.

M.J. Van Deventer
PERSIMMON HILL
Oklahoma City, OK

Chapter 5.
Preparing to Query

Respect the editors to whom you send your precisely targeted queries and typescripts. Send only your best pieces to hardworking, diligent editors who are inundated with typescripts and are faced with looming, dreadful deadlines; and your work will positively gleam.

Seeing Both Sides

Sometimes writers seem to forget that editors have lives, too. "A Day in the Life of an Editor," which Nancy McAlary and I have co-authored, allows you to peek in on fictionalized editor Barry Wesson and "put yourself in his shoes."

Barry Wesson perched on the chair in his doctor's office, fists clenched against his thighs as he waited to hear the results of his PSA test. But the frown on the doctor's face deepened and Barry knew, instinctively, it was bad news. Doc Wilson finally raised his head and looked directly at him, but before he could speak an explosive noise ripped through the room, and it was as though he were being lifted right off the chair. . . .

Barry's eyes flew open. Lightning crackled again, and a branch of the giant poplar right outside his bedroom window split and crashed to the ground.

"Great way to start the day," he muttered as he dragged himself out of bed. His feet had barely touched the floor when his son Andrew appeared in the bedroom doorway, shaking an empty cereal box at him.

"Dad! You said you were going to go shopping yesterday! There's nothing for breakfast!"

"I'll do it today," he said remorsefully. Then he remembered. First there were the editorial deadlines to meet, and at least one of his writers didn't have the promised article ready yet. Then later this afternoon he'd planned to visit his mother. He'd been putting it off, but he knew he was going to have to take a firm stand with her about selling her house and moving into an apartment. And of course, hanging like a threatening shadow over his entire day was that phone call from Doc Wilson. Today was the day the test results would be in.

"Oatmeal!" he announced to Andrew as he shrugged himself into his old robe and tried to sound undisturbed. "I know we have some oatmeal. It's just the thing you need for breakfast on a rainy morning like this!"

Within the half hour he'd put some semblance of order back into the chaos of his life. Andrew was soon bubbling with excitement about a field trip to the Mary Todd Lincoln House, and Barry had arranged for a lawn maintenance company to drop around later in the day to clean up the fallen branches out front.

On their way to school, the gas light came on. As Barry filled the tank, the rain started up again, pelting against him and driving his black wavy hair flat against his forehead. He threaded his way through traffic, dropped off Andrew at school, then finally reached his office during such a downpour that he could barely see his parking space.

As he hopped onto the elevator then strode the long corridor to the nest of offices that house *Show Horses* magazine, the aroma of ground roast coffee and hot glazed donuts wafted past reminding him that although he'd made sure Andrew had eaten, he hadn't taken time for his own breakfast.

Six hundred miles away Rebecca Stanfield had discovered that *Show Horses* magazine had not had an article on equine dental health listed in its index for the past year. She had learned from the guidelines—"Freelance articles welcome. Buys first N.A. serial print rights. Pays on acceptance. Competitive rates." She had found an abundance of library and internet resources for her proposed article. She knew she could arrange at least three interviews with vets specializing in equine care—one from Colorado, one from Kentucky, and one from South Carolina. Later she would call a stock photo place then drop her camera by the repair shop. But she felt sure she could prepare the piece, so she went online, cut and pasted her meticulous query into e-mail, proofed it one more time, then clicked "Send."

At 9:15 a.m. Barry grabbed a cup of black coffee and sank into his leather chair. Before he could gather his thoughts, he got a call from Madison MacArthur and even before Madison gave him the bad news, he sensed from the downbeat tone of the writer's voice what he was about to hear—that Madison wasn't going to be able to meet his deadline today for his assigned article for next month's issue due out next week.

During the next two hours, Barry met with his staff to outline a plan for their next six issues of *Show Horses*, interviewed a young woman for the mailroom position, and took a quick call from his broker. He also listened to his advertising department's presentation about their newest advertisers, and he examined samples of the tack accessories. Then he and his executive assistant, Angela, reviewed completed contracts from 17 writers, and he signed six checks. He made quick calls to his cover designer and to the print shop, and met, again, with his advertising group. Barry spoke quickly to the Red Cross Executive Director to confirm that he would continue as their chairperson for the upcoming fundraiser and that he definitely would be at the meeting tonight. He also took a call from the real estate agent who was searching for the perfect apartment for his mom.

At 11:40 a.m. Cassidy Elementary School called to say that Andrew was on his way to the emergency room at Eastern State Hospital. But before he could hear what had happened, the phone line went dead, a victim of the raging storm that was pounding the city.

By 11:50 a.m. Barry was at the hospital, anxiety coursing through him as he paced the corridor and waited to see the doctor who was attending Andrew. He forced himself to push back memories of the time he'd wrecked his bike and broken his arm. The hospital back then had seemed a cold, comfortless place, made worse by the fact that his father had abandoned them the year before; and his mom, slave to her factory job, couldn't get away to be with him until several hours later. When Andrew was born, Barry promised himself that he'd always be there for him, no matter what.

He whirled around at the sound of the examining room door opening. Before he could push the panicked words out to ask how Andrew was, the doctor gave him a reassuring smile. "It's just a cut," the doctor said. "It's deep and it took six stitches, but it's clean. It shouldn't even leave a scar."

Finally, the nurse helped Andrew into a wheelchair and pushed him down the corridor. Barry rushed to meet them and reached out for Andrew, who fought back his tears and said grim faced, "I missed going to Mary Todd Lincoln's House. . . ." Barry gave Andrew a bear hug and said, "I'm sorry. I promise I'll take you on Saturday."

By 1:00 p.m., Barry settled Andrew with Melissa Grant, his after-school sitter, and began the dash back downtown.

Just before 2:00 p.m., Barry bounded the stairs two at a time, raced through the automatic sliding glass doors, and rushed onto the elevator to pick up his day, or at least what was left of it. As he breezed by Angela's office, she called out, "Barry, I've ordered Mariachi Wrap for you from Chi Chi's. You've just gotta start taking time for yourself . . . ."

He interrupted, "Thanks. Steak, I hope."

"Yeah. Your favorite. But . . . ."

"Good. I'm starved," he said as he crossed the threshold of his office. Immediately, he called to check on Andrew. Then he asked Angela to give Red Cross a call to explain that he would not be attending the meeting this evening. "Please e-mail my report so that the executive director can present it, though, if you will." Trying to be nonchalant, he said, "Oh, yeah, and uhm, let me know as soon as Doc Wilson's office calls." Barry interviewed a young man for the mailroom position.

Then John Alexander, Barry's first reader, brought in four queries and two typescripts that he had chosen for "possible acceptance" out of more than 600 queries and 200 typescripts and placed them on Barry's desk. Together they went over the fine points and finally accepted one typescript and would send go-aheads for two of the queries.

Chi Chi's delivery boy, Tony Sylvester, brought in Barry's Mariachi Wrap, dropped it onto his desk, and took his payment and tip from a brandy snifter on the filing cabinet. Barry paused his conversation with John momentarily and said, "Thanks, Tony." He nodded and left quieter than he came. John picked up all the materials and, along with them, Barry's emergency note to call David Gallagher, a writer he always could count on during a jam.

Two hours later, Barry went into Angela's office to speak with the copy machine salesperson for a moment. Then he dictated a memo to Angela, and they went over a purchase order for supplies. As he rose, he asked her to call his travel agent to cancel his Saturday flight to Cheyenne. "I'll be taking Andrew to the Lincoln House instead. Oh, yeah, and please jot a reminder for me to get my mom a birthday gift before next Tuesday."

Still his day was not over. He conferred with a serious advertiser, and he interviewed another mailroom candidate. At 5:10 p.m., he finally folded down the paper on his, now cold, steak and took a bite as he checked his e-mail that Angela had screened and forwarded.

Message 13 intrigued him. Subject: Query— "Good Dental Care Protects Your Show Horse" From: Rebecca Stanfield. He remarked aloud, "Aha! Rebecca has read our magazine. Amazing! She's even followed our guidelines. . . ." His fingers flew across his keyboard to type— "Query interesting. Outline looks great. Your article is just what we need. E-mail it ASAP." Then he clicked "Send."

Six hundred miles away Rebecca tossed her fifth issue of *Music Everywhere!* onto the chair beside her, checked their published index of past articles, and said, "Woah. They haven't published a word about Tchaikovsky for two years."

During the next couple of hours, she previewed sources, arranged interviews, prepared her query "Tchaikovsky Forever," enclosed her sample publications "Brahms Revisited" and "Music for Your Angelfish," included her SASE for the editor's response, and sealed the packet to post tomorrow, because *Music Everywhere!* accepts submissions by post only.

At 6:15 p.m. Barry arrived home. The aroma of lasagna and homemade bread filled the air. As Melissa placed the dishes on the table, she said, "Well, I guess you're starved!"

"Actually, I had a very late lunch," said Barry. "You can hold dinner for a bit, if you don't mind. What I really am is exhausted."

"You push yourself too hard," Melissa chided. "You need to watch it or you'll end up sick." Worry flashed through him as Melissa's words reminded him that he hadn't heard from the doctor yet.

Barry sank onto the sofa beside Andrew, who was curled up soundly asleep. He stroked an errant strand of hair off his son's forehead.

"I think those painkillers the doctor gave him are still working," Melissa whispered as she handed Barry a glass of lemonade.

A surge of protective love raced over him as he studied his son's peaceful face.

"Poor little guy," he murmured. "He's had a rough day. He missed his field trip, but I'm going to make it up to him. It'll be the last breather I have before next week's deadlines. We've got this month's issue to get out, and the website to update." A list of "Things to Do" started to race through his mind and he continued to itemize them, barely aware that Melissa had moved back to the kitchen.

"And there's the Horse Writers' Association conference." He pulled off his shoes and stretched his legs across the ottoman as he curled his arm around Andrew. "Next week is going to be a rough one all right."

"But you'll manage," Melissa called from the kitchen. "You always do."

"I'll manage," Barry repeated as his eyes started to drift shut. They flew open almost immediately at the sound of the phone ringing, and he was already off the sofa when he heard Melissa repeat into the receiver "Doc Wilson's office? Sure thing. Just hold on a minute, and I'll get him."

"I'll manage," Barry said stoically to himself yet again as he reached to take the phone. "I always do."

In *Tales of a Traveller*, Washington Irving said, "I am always at a loss to know how much to believe my own stories." Well, this story easily depicts the truth. In fact, Barry's workday is light compared to the hectic days of many editors.

Consider what it must be like to be the real life editor of multiple publications. Such an editor is Anne Tullis, who serves as the Editor of *Golden Falcon*, Gulf Air's monthly inflight magazine, *Bahrain Gateway*, the official bi-monthly magazine of Bahrain International, *Oryx*, Qatar Air's bi-monthly inflight magazine, and *Oryx—Entertainment*, a bi-monthly inflight magazine, all under The Publishing Division of Promoseven Holdings of Bahrain. Nevertheless, within only a couple of days of requesting her participation in *TWF*, I received her gracious reply, "I am sorry to have taken so long to get back to you, but life has been far too hectic here."

Looking for Excellent Queries and Submissions

In the vignette above, Barry Wesson, needed one more article for his current month's issue with his deadline looming. Remember, Madison MacArthur telephoned at 9:15 a.m. to say that he would not be able to meet his deadline today. Wow! Rebecca Stanfield had impeccable timing, but timing was not her only advantage. Reexamine her approach with both *Show Horses* and with *Music Everywhere!* to see how she teams up with editors. Her method will work for you, too.

Studying Writer's Guidelines

In addition to editorial requirements such as deadlines, number of words, and documentation requirements, writer's guidelines will share information of importance to you such as pay rates, pay schedules [on acceptance, on publication, or number of weeks or months after publication] and how to submit your typescript—by hard copy only, by hard copy with disk (platform specified), by fax, by e-mail (as text in an e-mail message or sent as an attached file with platform indicated).

If your "target" magazine does not send out guidelines, check the most current market guides such as *Writer's Market, The Write Markets Report,* and *Gila Queen's Guide to Markets*, and also *Writers News* and *Writing Magazine,* to name a few, to find out as much information regarding submission to your "target" magazine as you can. *Writer's Digest* and *The Writer* also have up-to-the-minute market information. If you find an editor's listing on the internet requesting articles for an e-zine, often you can request writer's guidelines by e-mail. Many display their guidelines on their websites.

Understanding the Practicality of Querying

Most professional writers prefer to query first to save time and money. If you absolutely must submit sample clips with your query but you have none, then you have a problem. Do not fret. Find an editor who prefers to see a complete typescript. When you find such a publication that appeals to you, study several recent issues. Once you have done your homework and have a clear idea of a topic that will be of keen interest to the editor, submit a sparkling piece precisely according to your editor's guidelines. You, too, can have clips soon.

With your important homework completed, querying magazines that require queries before you write, though, can prevent you from expending your time and energy preparing articles on topics that may not fit into the plans of your target publication. Some editors like to be involved with the plan for your article. They offer valuable guidance that can help you not only with your current assignment for them, but also their suggestions often can help with your next sale to them and to other editors, as well. When you deal with publishers who require queries first, if you use the following suggestions carefully, they can help you to boost your sales to editors.

Getting Ready to Query

If your particular magazine runs an annual index, check it out, just as Rebecca did. In fact, check those for the past two or three years to see if it has been over a year or more since an article on a topic similar to yours was published. If you can introduce an exciting new angle to this perennial topic, you may have a winner. Now you just need to beat other writers to the punch with an especially strong query. If your magazine does not have its own index, check the *Reader's Guide to Periodical Literature* to see if your topic has appeared in your target magazine or other magazines.

Also, like Rebecca, you always should investigate before making a commitment. Do preliminary research to help narrow your topic and focus your theme. Visit the library or check out the internet for pertinent works to see how accessible information is on the fascinating slant of your topic.

Continue your search and notetaking until you are sure that you will be able to develop an article. It is of utmost importance to be able to deliver what you promise. You do not want to make the mistake that the fictionalized character Madison MacArthur made.

Also, find the names, postal addresses, e-mail addresses, telephone, and fax numbers of authorities you can interview for up-to-the-minute data. Line up interviews with experts from a broad geographical range.

Think through some useful questions to guide your preparation.

• What new information will you be able to share with readers?

- How will the information impact their lives?
- What lead time are you considering for your article?
- What is the lead time of your target publication? Keeping in mind the magazine's anticipated response time, can you match its lead time effectively?
- From the day of your go-ahead, how much time will you need to prepare your piece and to have it in your editor's hands? When you make your promise, give yourself some buffer time to cover emergencies.
- Does your target publication prefer postal submissions or e-mail submissions?
- Is your publication local, regional, national, or international? If the editor does not permit e-mail submissions, you must remember to take into consideration the location of the publisher and give ample time for the postal service or use overnight delivery services. In any event, plan to meet your deadline in advance, if possible. It will make your editor happy to receive your work a bit early.
- Do you feel confident that you can develop your article in accordance with the word limit of your target publication?
- Do you feel confident about your research findings and potential contributions from experts you will interview?
- Have you written other articles on other aspects of your topic?

Buying Business Basics Stationery

Even your stationery is important when you query print magazine or newspaper editors. You want even your envelope and your stationery to make a good first impression. You can purchase good quality, white bond letterheads with matching envelopes and business cards inexpensively from a fine print shop. Have your name and address printed in a business font that appeals to you and that will appeal to editors, too. Have the printer use black ink. Underneath your name in much smaller print, you can—if you choose—have your writing specialty printed such as "Sports Writer" or "Travel Writer." Avoid fanciful logos—quills, typewriters, and computers. Get business basics. Busy editors do not have time for annoying excesses.

Get estimates from about three print shops on the exact same materials of your choice—paper and fonts—then take the best deal. Often the prices vary extremely from print shop to print shop.

If you use a laser printer, you simply may choose to print your name and address, e-mail address, fax and phone numbers in a reasonable size and a suitable font and layout of your choice at the top of your cotton bond paper at the same time that you print your outgoing letters.

You will feel good about your choices, and you will be more confident as you send out your queries and later your cover letters for the many "go-ahead" articles that you will write. Like Rebecca, you will have your opportunity, too!

• • •

Chapter 6. Composing a Sparkling Query Letter

Open your query letter with a knock-your-socks-off statistic, question or quote, or a confounding comparison or contrast. Whatever your start—an allusion or comparison or contrast, a problem, a question, or an explanation—your start must be striking.

Sometimes creating a captivating title early can help you to develop your theme statement and your introduction to help focus your work. Incorporate your intriguing title in the first or second paragraph of your query. Titles that titillate work best. My friend, Ray Bronk, sold an article to *Field & Stream* with the beguiling title "Good Camouflage Is Hard to Find."

Some writers open their query letters with a hook prepared for the introduction of their first draft. Be able to support your captivating hook with anecdotes, if your publication uses them, as well as quotes, statistics, and other information of substance from reliable sources on both sides of your issue.

Succinctly summarize what you propose to cover. Be sure to enumerate the top experts who have agreed to contribute their knowledge and expertise for your article. Tell your editor why the information that you will present is important enough to be published. Also tell your editor the number of words you will supply as per her guidelines and the date you will have it on her desk.

If your target magazine is photo-driven and writers listed in the masthead are credited with the photos, then be ready to furnish photos for your article. Note what your editor prefers—black and white glossy prints, color transparencies, or electronic format—and tell her you can provide such images.

Querying Well

Your query letter is a bit like an audition. Your goal is to convey that you have the confidence required to track down information, conduct interviews, analyze materials, and present information with clarity in an interesting way. Place yourself and your topic in the spotlight to intrigue the editor and to clarify why you are the excellent candidate to write the article to enlighten or entertain readers. However, avoid being overzealous or overconfident.

Your well-written query on a unique or unusual topic is one of your main keys to success. Your query should show your editor that you have read and understand her magazine, that you can follow instructions, and that you are prepared to cooperate to fullfil the requirements of her publication. Queries save you time and help you to earn more money. You will not waste time preparing articles that editors do not want.

Self-Editing Your Query

Become "the editor," and ask yourself these questions about "the writer" of the query. Remain as objective as you can. Get rid of any errors that have sneaked into your work.

- Has "this writer" confined the query to a single page? It is important to keep the query to the standard single page. A succinct query shows a great deal about how well you can handle materials.

- Has "this writer" typed absolutely correctly the name and address of the specific editor to whom the work should go?

- Has "this writer" offered a specific article for sale, and does it match its target market?

Addressing a Specific Editor by Formal Name

If you will be able to produce what you promise, write a query letter to the magazine's managing editor or to the designated contact person as stated in your market guide or writer's guidelines. If the editor holds a Ph.D. or M.D. degree, greet that editor by the title "Dr." plus the last name. If the editor simply could be addressed as Mr. or Ms. but the name is one such as "Chris" Alexander, which is used for both males and females, telephone the editorial office and ask the administrative assistant whether you should use Mr., Ms., or Mrs. to address the editor. You can address the editor as "Dear Editor Alexander" or "Dear Chris Alexander" if you are hesitant about calling. In such cases, check the masthead of the most recent issue of your target magazine to be sure that you have the name of the appropriate editor for your submission.

Debbie Ridpath Ohi, Editor of *Inklings*, who has shared ideas in Chapters 2 and 3, says, "I appreciate authors who make the effort to spell my name correctly and who send their queries to the right e-mail address."

Editors vary in their styles of greetings and conducting business, and although some enjoy informality, it probably is best to greet them formally, yet friendly enough so as not to be seen as stuffy. Be genuine and respectful. Many editors will set the level of formality.

Some e-zine editors conduct business on a first-name basis right away. You can follow your editor's lead regarding a proper greeting. Your respect still can be conveyed in your e-mail messages and in your diligence to produce quality articles on time.

There is no excuse ever to misspell the editor's name. If the name of the editor to whom you are about to submit your query or finished typescript is spelled one way in the writer's guidelines and another in the masthead of the magazine, you can call the editorial office and ask the administrative assistant for clarification. If you have been following the magazine for some time, you may see your familiar editor leave and another one come aboard. Pay close attention to these changes. Avoid submitting your work to the name of an editor who left the magazine six months ago. Editors are not pleased to receive submissions addressed to a previous editor.

Occasionally, an editor's name will run through the time of that editor's preparation of issues, even though he has taken a position elsewhere. Finally, though, the new editor's name will be listed in the masthead. If you read the editorial changes reported in market guides such as *The Write Markets Report* and *Gila Queen's Guide to Markets*, they can help you to stay on top of these important situations when you are trying to establish a smooth working relationship with editors.

In fact, if you feel passionately about your query and you are burning with desire to be published in a particular magazine, then, for the small price of a quick phone call to the editorial office, you can have the administrative assistant or an assistant editor clarify that the editor to whom you are about to submit your work still is in command. It is as simple as that.

Continuing to Examine Your Query

Do you—as the editor you now are role-playing—like what you see? If not, why? Mark the corrections that must be made to improve the work. About the mechanics and the development of your query, ask yourself the following questions.

- Does the text appear aesthetically pleasing?
- Does the cotton bond paper and your mono-spaced font present a clean image?
- Are your margins at least one to one and one-half inches on all sides?

In general, editors do not seem to like justified right margins. If your editor requests a justified right margin, then follow his instructions. If not, do not justify the right margin.

- Is the beginning sentence clear and captivating?
- Does the query intrigue you?
- Can you read "this writer's" letter with ease?
- Are the grammar, spelling, and punctuation in this letter correct, and are they conveyed in an appropriate tone?
- Are the paragraphs well-developed, yet succinct?
- Do you know which experts or celebrities "the writer" will interview?

Quoting Respected Authorities

For my article, "Surgery is not the only remedy for cataracts," published in *Green Farm Magazine* in the United Kingdom, I was able to offer that I would quote from James Heffley, Ph.D., the editor of *The Journal of Applied Nutrition*, Austin, Texas, Allen Taylor, Ph.D., Director of the Lens Nutrition and Aging Division of the U.S. Department of Agriculture Research Center of Aging at Tufts University, Boston, Massachusetts, and G. Edwin Bunce, Ph.D., and John L. Hess, Ph.D., of the Department of Biochemistry and Nutrition at the Virginia Polytechnic Institute and State University, Blacksburg, Virginia, to explain the significance of nutrition in the delay of the onset of cataracts.

Still in your role as an editor, continue with the following questions about your query.

- Do you sense a spirit of cooperation and confidence from the words of "this writer"?
- What special insight or experience does "this writer" possess that will make this article one to remember?
- Will your audience want to read "this writer's" article?
- Why is "this writer" the perfect candidate for this particular article?

Presenting Your Credentials

Describe a bit about your published works. Give your credentials. If you do not have any bylines yet, just do not mention bylines. Provide relevant information that supports you as a writer for your intended article. If your article is about learning to ride horses, and you are a seasoned equestrian [or equestrienne], then say so. Continue to work with care, and soon you will have clips.

Still reading as if you are an editor, ask yourself the following questions about your query.

- Do you know what the query proposes and how "the writer" plans to handle the preparation of the article?
- Why will "this writer's" work impact the reader?
- Does "this writer" know the word limit?

Furnishing Photos

- Will "this writer" supply photos?

If you can supply black and white glossy prints or color transparencies, inform the editor. Again rely on your writer's guidelines and useful references, then offer exactly what the editor requires. You can say something such as, "I can have this 1000-word article complete with B&W glossy prints, as per your preference, on your desk within three weeks."

Supplying a Sidebar

- Ask yourself, will "this writer" supply a sidebar?

If you can send a sidebar of useful information pertinent to your topic, let the editor know.

Now ask yourself—

- How soon will "this writer" complete the article?
- Does "this writer" supply clips?

Sending Clips with Your Query

You may remember Sara Gilbert, the Editor of *U.S. Art*, from Chapter 3, "Finding Your Dream Publications." Gilbert says, "Send your finest clip along with your first query so that the editor knows both that you have been published and how well you write."

If you have articles online supportive to your proposed topic, give the titles of a couple of your best articles along with their correct URLs. Double check the URLs to make sure that you have given them correctly to make the editor's review of your articles a pleasant experience.

- Do you feel from the essence of the query that "this writer" will meet the deadline?

After reading "this writer's" query and thinking through these questions and others that may come to mind, answer this question,

Would you assign this topic to "this writer"?

If you noticed some weak spots, then modify your query letter. Improve it. Work on it until it truly is ready to submit. Finally, print out your improved version and proofread it. Correct any typographical errors or transpositions or repeated words. Supply any inadvertently omitted words. Print your final copy. Proof it. Submit it. Now glide along to your next project, and be patient. Soon you may receive a go-ahead.

Saving Postage

To save postage, you may prefer to send a #10 self-addressed, stamped envelope (SASE) for the editor's reply and indicate in your brief cover letter that your typescript need not be returned, when submitting on speculation to publications that prefer typescripts rather than queries. Always send a fresh, clean, specifically targeted copy to any editor to whom you submit your work.

If you believe that a "no-return of your typescript request" conveys that you do not care about your work, you may prefer to pay for the extra postage. Some journals, though, require multiple copies of your submission—one original and two copies. Such a policy can add considerably to your business expenses, especially when you supply two-way postage.

Once you have numerous publishing credits, you will feel more comfortable enclosing with your query or typescript a mere stamped, self-addressed post card or SASE for the editor's response. With the ideal situation, your material will not need to be returned. Your work will be accepted and published.

Using E-Mail Saves Time and Money

As more and more publications go online and request that submissions be embedded in e-mail or sent as e-mail attachments, writers will appreciate enormous savings over hard copy mailings.

Asking for a Response

In closing, ask for a response. You might say, "SASE enclosed. I will look forward to hearing from you." Never pressure the editor for a prompt response. With your query sent through the postal service, most publications require you to send a self-addressed, stamped envelope for the editor's response.

Using a Polite Closing

Use a polite closing such as "Best regards" or "Kindest regards" or "Sincerely yours," then sign your full name, if posting a hard copy by regular mail. Even though e-mail messages tend to be less formal, a polite closing in e-mail can be just as important with some editors who like them.

Think through your query, compose it, rework it, proofread it, and polish it to make it sparkle, and your editor will look forward to receiving other queries from you. Remember your query introduces you to your editor. Now slide your query letter into a crisp, clean envelope that you have addressed with the utmost care.

Receiving a "Go-Ahead"

First names often are used in e-mail messages, but when a printed materials editor returns a handwritten note and uses your first name, even if it is a rejection, that very well may be a good sign. Continue to study the magazine and query with a different idea soon. Perhaps the next time, you will get a "go-ahead." With persistence, concentration of efforts, and definiteness of purpose, you surely will succeed.

Gilbert of *U.S. Art* advises, "Be persistent but not overbearing. Don't pretend to know the magazine's audience better than the editor."

Responding to the "Go-Ahead"

Make sure to print your article on cotton bond paper on one side of the paper only. Never submit your work on onionskin or erasable bond. Use black ink and a letter quality or laser printer.

To make the important point that no so-called rules or suggestions always apply, you should know that to encourage recycling and the wise use of resources, Robert N. Stephenson, Editor of *Altair* in Blackwood, S.A., Australia, allows writers to submit their science fiction stories on the backs of sheets of paper used for an earlier typescript.

Policies change. Editors move from one publication to another. So before submitting any work to Stephenson, though, study *Altair's* most current guidelines to be sure that he still abides by that policy.

For years, it has been safe to say, "Never fold your typescript like a letter and stuff it into a #10 envelope." However, Kathryn Ptacek's *The Gila Queen's Guide to Markets* 86, Spring 1997, reported that *The Beloit Poetry Journal* says, "Use regular business envelopes (4 x 9). Don't worry about creases. Wasteful manila envelopes with excess postage just make us sad."

While most publishers would frown upon receiving paper with print on both sides or receiving an article, story, or poem that has been folded and stuffed into a regular business size envelope, obviously, not every publisher does.

Following the Instructions of Your Specific Editor

For best results, the important point, then, is to follow exactly the instructions of the editor for whom you wish to write. This point cannot be overemphasized.

Most often, though, typescripts require 9 x 12 or 10 x 13 mailers. These sizes work well together. If your typescript is thin enough to fit into a 9 x 12 envelope, you can slip your stamped, self-addressed 9 x 12 return envelope (SASE) into the 10 x 13 outgoing envelope without any need to fold it.

Note that the guidelines may request a self-addressed envelope (SAE) and postage. If so, then send a self-addressed envelope, but do not affix the stamps to the return mailer. Instead, place the stamps into a small envelope along with your work. Attention to detail will serve you.

Some writers suggest that it is passé to send the SAE and international reply coupons (IRCs) to editors abroad. Considering the words of Jim Adair of Canada and G.W. Amick of Spain in Chapter 4, "Knowing Your Audience," certainly some editors still do want proper return postage (SAE with IRCs) supplied. Again, study the writer's guidelines of your target magazine to know what your particular editor requires. Be prudent. Supply what is requested. Indeed, once you have an ongoing relationship with an editor who publishes your work consistenly, return postage probably will no longer be necessary. Until then, be judicious.

Seeing Your Sales Soar

A provocative, get-to-the-point query written smoothly in a friendly tone can earn that elusive "go-ahead" sooner than you may have imagined, and your publications will soar.

Each time you receive a check and a complimentary copy of your published article, send a polite thank-you note to the editor. Along with that thank-you, submit your next sparkling query letter. Happy sales!

Skeleton Query Letter

Your Letterhead
Date

Exact Name and Correct Title of Your Particular Target Editor
Correct and Complete Address including zip code

Salutation [Be absolutely certain that you use the editor's correct title.]

Dear Ms. _____:
Dear Mr. _____:
Dear Dr. _____:

Paragraph One—Your Lead

* Interest the editor with one of the following time-tested leads—
  * a remarkable anecdote (if her magazine uses them)
  * an extraordinary definition
  * an intriguing question
  * a startling fact or statistic
  * a compelling quote
  * a commonplace happening with a new twist
  * an unparalleled event
  * a thought-provoking comparison or contrast
  * a reference to a celebrity
  * a reference to a news event
* Give specific information on the topic you are proposing.
* Include your working title for your article if you can do so smoothly.

Paragraph Two—Your Promise

* Summarize the slant of your article.
* Outline the key points you promise to cover in your article.
* Include facts, figures, and research to support your proposal.
* If pertinent, mention important sources you will use.
* If you can produce bold new interviewees and experts who will participate, name them.

*   If your article has a peg, you can suggest it. If there are special reasons that your topic is timely, explain why.

*   If your proposed article follows up on and supports previous articles of the publication, indicate that it does.

*   Explain to the editor why your article will serve her audience.

*   Explain your new twist. What sets your article apart from previous articles on your topic?

Paragraph Three—Your Clarification of Mechanics
[You show that you will follow your editor's instructions.]

*   Identify the rights you are selling.

*   Define the projected length of your article according to your editor's requirements.

*   State whether you will submit photos, illustrations, or charts to support your text.

*   If you can offer sidebars, say so. Many editors appreciate sidebars and pay well for them.

*   Let your editor know how soon you can have your article on her desk.

Paragraph Four—Your Credentials and Experience

*   Sell yourself.

*   Outline your credentials being careful to be neither boastful nor bashful.

*   If you have special qualifications for writing your proposed article, say so. Do not mention writing classes you have taken, however.

*   If you have not yet received a byline, do not mention it. Instead, just continue to work to receive bylines.

*   If you have published several articles, mention two or three that most closely relate to your query.

*   If clips are required with your query, send two or three of yours that demonstrate you can write about your proposed topic.

Finally,

*   Ask to write the article.

*   Ask for a response.

Closing
[Choose from a selection of polite closings.]

Best regards,

Kind regards,

Sincerely yours,

Very truly yours,

[When you hear from your editor and develop a relationship with her, you may choose to use the closing that she prefers. The smoother you can make your communication with editors, the greater your chances for success.]

Sign your full name

[Your query is your offer to sell your article. After you develop a friendship with an editor, you most likely will sign only your first name.]

If you are not using letterhead, then after you sign your name in black ink, type your
Full Name
Full Address
Telephone number
Fax number
E-mail address

Enclosures.

Self-addressed, stamped envelope (SASE)

[The SASE is a must with many editors. Foster your relationship with editors by being cooperative.]

Clips or tear sheets

[Include clips or tear sheets, if required.]

Sample Query Letter

Linda Davis Kyle
P.O. Box 10000 City, State zip

January 2, 2004
Amelia Stone, Editor
Writing for Tomorrow
2000 Writing Way
Omaha, Nebraska zip

Re: Capturing That Elusive Go-Ahead

Dear Ms. Stone:

Recently, Jan Werblin, the Associate Editor of *Professional Counselor Magazine*, sent me an e-mail message which read:

> Thanks, Linda. I really appreciate your prompt reply and professionalism. It's wonderful to work with you.
>
> Jan

Being on good terms with the editor of one's target magazine is a writer's dream come true. In "Capturing That Elusive Go-Ahead," a two-part article, I will provide a blueprint for writers to help build enduring and fulfilling relationships with editors. In "Step One: Preparing to Query," I will point out the importance of referring to the most up-to-date market guides. I will explain rights. I will address the importance of preliminary research to determine a dynamite topic and the absolute necessity of analyzing the target publication and its advertisements. I will discuss creating a catchy title and grabbing an editor's attention. In "Step Two: Querying," I will begin with an attention-grabbing lead and go on to discuss the importance of a compelling promise. Finally, I will invite aspiring writers to explore paragraph by paragraph an easy method to prepare successful queries.

As per your requirements, I can supply both 2000-word typescripts for First N.A. serial print rights within three weeks of your request. I also can supply a sidebar of useful writing books published within the last six months.

My articles on writing have appeared in *Canadian Writer's Directory, Gila Queen's Guide to Markets, The Write Markets Report,* and *The Write Way,* to name a few.

I look forward to hearing from you. SASE enclosed.

Best regards,

Linda Davis Kyle

Enclosures.

Note: This imaginary query has not been submitted to *Writing for Tomorrow*; however, my article "Capturing that Elusive 'Go-Ahead'" was published in *Canadian Writer's Directory* in Victoria, B.C., Canada, in January 1992. Editor Gordon M. Smart wrote to me, "We have received other pieces on this subject [writing queries], but yours are better written and more specific. It is a pleasure to see material professionally prepared and submitted."

As a bit of a digression, keep in mind that sometimes you even can receive assignments without querying. When I e-mailed Jan to ask permission to include her note to me in this book, she not only responded with, "Of course you may use my comments to you. I am happy to be able to help," but also she said, "By the way, would you like another assignment? I'm sure I've got something here for you."

Now that is a writer's dream come true! Remember, respecting your editors will reward you with assignment after assignment.

Editors appreciate excellent writers, so target carefully and responsibly, and become an editor's dream come true. Donna Welsh, Production Editor of *WellBeing* in Sydney, NSW, Australia, whom you first met in Chapter 2, "Getting on the Right Track," says, "All articles appearing in *WellBeing* are written by professionals in their fields or professionl writers—without them we would not have a magazine."

When you do query and do so successfully, you will receive a go-ahead to prepare your article. Then you will get to prepare a companion letter to accompany your submission.

Cover Letters

With your submission, you will want to include a brief cover letter simply to introduce your completed work to your editor. After the proper name, title, correct address, and proper greeting with your editor's name spelled correctly, you can say something such as

Dear Jan:

My approximate 1500-word Mike Levine Q & A article follows for your April 1999 issue of *Professional Counselor Magazine*, as promised, in advance of your December 1998 deadline.

I hope that this article will interest and benefit your readers.

Best regards,

Linda

Guy Lancaster of *The Arkansas Review*, whom you first met in Chapter 3, "Finding Your Dream Publications," says, "It is perhaps depressing and insulting to our artistic integrity, but writers have to know how to sell their work. I once received a poetry submission that included a three-stanza poem with a two-page cover letter in which the author told me everything about the poem—what his mood was, why he chose certain words, and what personal meaning a particular line held for him. Cover letters with such extraneous information simply irritate editors. If a work is worth publishing, it will stand on its own without the author's lengthy comments, and in the almost impenetrable world of publishing, it is not beneficial to give the editor a reason to dislike you."

Happy querying!

• • •

Chapter 7.
Maximizing Your Research

Read widely on your chosen topic to begin with a panoramic view. The more you know about your topic, the better you will be able to filter your abundant collection of information into your finished article. Once you have studied many issues of your target publication and you know its audience, what your editor wants, and your topic with its special slant or theme, you can narrow the focus of your research.

You can look into the history of your chosen topic with its unique slant and carry the subject all the way to its current status, if it suits your target publication.

M.J. Van Deventer, the Editor of *Persimmon Hill* magazine, whom you met in Chapter 2, "Getting on the Right Track," says, "Historical accuracy is of the utmost importance for our publication." You can include historical accounts from sources such as diaries, journals, and pertinent autobiographies.

At the other end of the spectrum, if your target publication is more interested in exciting breakthroughs in the computer industry or the medical industry—or a blending of the two—you might discover experts with the best credentials, who can make predictions about the futures of these fields.

Finding Prominent Authorities

Find the most prominent authorities on your topic. Read from as many of their works as possible. Find out how their colleagues view these experts and their work. When you interview experts, find the most objective ones that you can. Keep in mind that almost everyone has an agenda. When an issue is split, interview sources from both sides. Your goal will be to find the truth as well as you can.

In your search through reputable resources of all kinds, you will unearth information to find answers to questions such as what has happened with your topic, and what initiated the situation, problem, or condition? You will evaluate what is happening with your topic currently and what influences it and what it influences. You will try to anticipate what will be happening with your chosen topic—what can ignite it and what can snuff it out.

Being Confident of Ample Materials

When you find avenues to be able to answer all these basics, you can feel safe to write your query and submit it. When you have collected your materials, you have many choices for organizing them logically. You may choose to develop your article chronologically or hierarchically. You may prioritize. You may describe and develop your article by moving the reader from general information to specific information or from specific data to general notions. You may lead your reader through how-to steps or procedures to enlighten or to entertain. You even may introduce a topic and follow an alphabetized list or a numerical list, if it works for your particular material. In addition, you can organize by cause and effect, just to name a few approaches. Once you have organized your information by a method that works for you and have a working outline of categories and subcategories, you will know that you can compose and deliver what you promise. On-time delivery is a must for successful writing.

During your preliminary research, you also can collect the names and postal addresses, e-mail addresses, and phone numbers of authorities whom you possibly can interview to supplement your library and internet data.

If you can line up interview appointments with some experts prior to sending your editor a query, be sure to tell him. Having willing prospective interviewees on the level to match your publication can enhance your chances to get that important go-ahead to write your article. For a local publication, published within the boundaries of your own city, you may prefer that your interviewees be residents of your area. For a regional publication, a more prominent authority may be helpful. For national and international publications, experts of national and international renown will be most useful.

Researching with Multiple Purposes in Mind

Before you begin your full-fledged research to produce one article, you can formulate your approach to cover several diverse angles on your chosen topic. At first, you may choose to research only two different aspects of your subject. As you advance, though, you may collect information in one long research session for as many as four or five articles.

Still, you will want to stay well focused on each of your individual slants. Staying alert for key words that pop up repeatedly will help you to begin to recognize good possibilities for additional slants. Paying close attention to your target magazine's bent also can help you to discover areas that are likely to work. As you gain experience, the task of collecting information on multiple angles becomes easier. You will know exactly which of your target magazines will welcome your proposed topics.

Offering Some Examples

Let's say that you already have received your go-ahead to write on eye care and safety for a magazine for parents of youngsters ages three to 10. It is merely a step away to uncover loads of useful information on eye care and safety for the mature population.

Ophthalmologists can speak equally authoritatively on vision problems specific to youth and specific to mature patients, and they can inform you about vision problems, eye care, and eye safety common to both groups.

Be sure to read from many sources and collect information from topnotch medical journals available in your nearest library and on the internet. Then prepare thoughtful, logical questions that your experts may actually enjoy answering. They will be able to cover a great deal of ground with up-to-the-minute data. Your authorities can share their information with both charm and vigor. Their interview answers can captivate readers and, at the same time, substantiate claims that you have encountered in your collection of materials. If prodded, they even may present their predictions or dramatic inner thoughts. Many experts enjoy sharing information about what their particular profession offers. Many love sharing their passion for their life's work.

You can use different aspects of information from the same authority for different slants for different magazines. Just be sure to remember to ask your expert a wide range of questions so that you have plenty of gold nugget quotes for each slant you are covering on your wider, all-encompassing "umbrella" topic. As you prepare your assignment such as "Guarding Youngsters' Precious Vision," you also can collect information to pitch a new query to a magazine dedicated to serving readers ready for bifocals.

You could ask your ophthalmologist interviewee such questions as—

- What is the latest treatment for glaucoma in adults?

  (Children also get glaucoma, under some circumstances, such as trauma to the eye. So sometimes, even if you confine your question, the ophthalmologist may expound beyond your limits. For your purposes, this extra information will be excellent.)

- Besides laser surgery, what is the latest treatment for cataracts?

- Have you done any personal research on the prevention of macular degeneration through optimum nutrition?

- What are the most common vision problems experienced by toddlers?

If you have read a great deal on your topic, you will be able to ask better questions. Avoid asking questions that can be answered with a "yes" or "no." Especially, ask your interviewee questions whose answers will enable you to provide the readers with data they may not have read anywhere else before.

Seeing Ubiquitous Possibilities

As you become more accustomed to researching several different slants simultaneously, you will start to see possibilities everywhere. When you research to generate an article such as "Keeping Mature Eyes Safe," you could prepare to write an article on safety goggles worn for sports, safety eyeglasses used in chemistry laboratories, and wraparounds worn to do landscaping and lawn work. From the internet, you can "click" up an abundance of information on fashionable eyewear—sunglasses, gradient-tinted lenses, and colored contact lenses. No longer will you be writing some piddling little article now and then. Instead, suddenly your writing projects will become a clamoring, rowdy crowd elbowing themselves to the front of the line for you to finish them.

Achieving Your Goals

With the well-defined goal to find very specifically targeted information, you can find an incredible number of possibilities for articles. You will have an abundance of useful information to share with your readers. Your research sessions can take a bit more time, and you must be a bit more methodical in your approach; but if you manage your time and your materials carefully and professionally, you can count on greater earnings, as well. Happy researching!

• • •

Chapter 8.
Interviewing and Beyond

If you have been a professor of botany for the past 12 years and you decide to write about "The Role of Chloroplasts in the Process of Photosynthesis," you may not need to read a great number of reference materials to write your article. If you have been a runway model for six years, you may not need to interview designers and other models to write "Dressing to Look Your Best." You may have more than enough information from firsthand experience. You may be the expert on the subject.

Interviewing Experts from a Wide Geographic Range

If you are not the expert on a subject, you simply will need to support your own storehouse of experience and knowledge with research materials and interviews to give the depth and extra dimension to develop your article. If you are writing the article for a U.S. magazine, it is a good idea, if possible, to interview about three experts—one from the West coast, one from the Heartland, and one from the East coast—by e-mail, by phone, or in person.

Interviewing Experts from Several Countries

As you advance and write for international audiences, it is a good idea to share information from two or three international experts—either from their books, journal articles, or by interview by means of e-mail, postal service, or phone. It is best to avoid the use of faxes unless you have been invited to fax the person. Based on your relationship with the expert, you will determine which method is the most courteous and least intrusive to set up an appointment for an interview.

Acquiring Interviews—The Hard Way

If you do not know the person, using the postal service may be the least intrusive way to request a time for an interview. To encourage a reply, be sure to include a stamped, self-addressed envelope or a self-addressed envelope and international reply coupons, if applicable. If you send your interview questions along to the expert or celebrity, a few will respond by return postal mail or by e-mail.

Because people are bombarded constantly with everything from requests for money for fundraisers to "come-on" advertising of every imaginable sort, the chance of a reply to your postal letter is decidedly slim. Often experts who are somewhat out of the limelight will give their time generously even to total strangers, but those still "in the glow" will have either a service who gives a form reply, or you may receive no reply. If you can convince the service of your seriousness and your noble intentions, you may be lucky enough finally to interview your expert or celebrity. Patience and persistence, in most cases, will be required, though.

If you know the person slightly or have a friend who does, or you belong to the same local, regional, national, or international organization, you may feel comfortable to contact the person by phone or by e-mail to set up a convenient time for the interview. Be sure to mention your connection. Also, be prepared at that time you call to conduct an interview. The person may invite you to proceed with the interview immediately. Dr. Michael Scott of Sierra Tucson, who is listed in *The Best Doctors in America: Pacific Region,* gave a beautiful off-the-cuff interview during our first conversation for a recent assignment of mine, "Alternative Treatments for Addictions: Promises and Perils." So do not miss a great chance to complete your mission posthaste.

Recognizing a "Catch-22" Situation

Of course, it would be easier to receive an assignment from a magazine editor, if you could say, in your query letter, that you will interview "Nobel Prize winner _____," or "Olympic champion _____," or "Pulitzer prize winner _____." Likewise, it would be easier to engage the participation of the Nobel Prize winner (in a chosen category), or a recent Olympic champion, whom you admire, or a Pulitzer prize winner, who is your favorite author, if you have acquired a go-ahead from your target magazine. If you could say at the outset of your e-mail, letter, or phone call that you would like to interview the individual for your article on "The Five Top _____ Winners of the Century" that will be published in an upcoming issue of the *XYZ Magazine,* landing the interview is exceedingly promising. Of course, it helps win over the interviewee if you already have an assignment.

A partial solution to this problem is to locate a recognized expert in your own city and arrange to conduct a face-to-face interview. Often, the promise of such an interview can help to gain the assignment and help to add other experts who will want to contribute information later.

Being Wise

If your article is about a primary source such as the celebrity, expert, or eyewitness being interviewed, then obviously the interview with that individual is quite necessary. However, in other cases you have more flexibility. If you are exploring to find information on natural remedies to ward off depression; or if you want to find the latest word on exotic cars, there are an

The Writer's Friend

abundance of qualified health care professionals whom you can ask for the first interview and plenty of exotic car experts whom you can consult for the latter interview.

Find interviewees with impeccable credentials. Read about authorities in the field of your chosen topic.

- What is your interviewee's reputation among his colleagues?
- Is he respected among his peers? What are his major accomplishments?

It often will work well to interview several experts for each article. If all your experts give sterling answers and great quotable quotes and all confirm their quotes, if needed, in a timely fashion—terrific. In reality, though, not all experts give sparkling information. You will not want to add information that contributes nothing new to your article. You will not want to include drab quotes that add no zest to your article just because an expert said it.

Some experts also may not be available if you need to double check their quotes. If your deadline for submission is grabbing you by the ankles, you can omit any questionable information given by one of your experts if you cannot get clarification from the person in your allotted time. With the information that you have from your other interviewees you still can have ample information to develop your article.

If your interviewee is a witness to a phenomenon, listen to her viewpoint and note her special ways of expressing her feelings. Note sources she mentions beyond her actual eyewitness account. Does she have access to private materials such as letters and diaries?

Sideline Interviewing

Sometimes sideline interviews can add sparkle to your work. Interviewing the father of a famous sports figure could add an extra dimension to your article on the renowned sports figure. Interviewing an old school chum of the athlete can add new insight and new interpretation. So do not forget to seek out these other sources when they are relevant.

Finding Other Avenues

In the event that you can line up neither the interviews that you first intended nor the assignment, do not give up. You can find other experts who will share their ideas and their important research findings. You also can query a different target magazine.

You simply can dig out some of the information you need from useful, up-to-date library sources. Also from the vast array of internet sources, you can make prudent selections for reliable materials. Document your sources—

books, journals, online information, and statements made in earlier published interviews that you have read—and be sure to surround any verbatim materials with quotation marks. If any inaccurate bit of information happens to appear, your reader can trace it to its original source.

Keep an accurate accounting of your specific sources for your own records, even if your particular target magazine does not require precise documentation with footnotes and literature cited. You can be served well by careful records.

Recently, when a potential investor wanted to know the documentation for one of my articles for *BodyIsland*, I was able to supply Ed Starkie, the Website Coordinator, with the needed information within minutes of receiving his request.

Acquiring Interviews—The Easy Way

Using PR Newswire, NEWSdesk, and ProfNet

Certainly, one way to take the worry out of lining up experts for interviews is to land solid assignments then acquaint yourself with the excellent services of PR Newswire, including the PRN Press Room, NEWSdesk, and ProfNet. Within hours, you literally can be inundated with responses from PR services offering interviews with outstanding researchers and other experts from across the country and around the world.

Recently, within 12 hours of submitting a ProfNet query for one of my assignments, I received invitations straight from 17 top experts, who generously offered to be interviewed, or messages from their representatives, who supplied the credentials of the experts along with thoughtful offers to set up interviews for me. PR Newswire, NEWSdesk, and ProfNet are indispensable tools for today's writers who are interested in presenting cutting edge information. Now your articles can sparkle with up-to-the-minute information.

Introducing an Unparalleled Way to Improve Your Articles

Renu Aldrich, Public Relations Manager of PR Newswire, based in New York city, shares the following information. PR Newswire is the world leader in the electronic distribution of news releases to the media and financial community, having founded the industry 45 years ago. With its 29 U.S. bureaus, five overseas bureaus, an exclusive partnership with Canada NewsWire and its vast network of wire, fax, internet, satellite, and e-mail delivery, PRN serves the news release needs of public relations and investor relations professionals worldwide. PR Newswire offers its 33,000 customers a variety of options for distributing news releases and images, from worldwide dissemination of news releases to the targeting of specific journalists and other audiences through wire, fax, internet, and e-mail. All wire distribution options satisfy SEC disclosure requirements and include distribution to hundreds of premier internet-based databases, online services and trading sites such as Yahoo!, AOL, and PointCast with links back to company websites, product information, and e-commerce opportunities.

Companies and organizations also use PR Newswire to enhance their internet presence with online news release and photo archives, audio and video cybercasts of conference calls, press conferences and events, and maintenance-free investor relations websites that dramatically reduce the time required to respond to current and prospective investors.

PR Newswire reaches more than 22,000 global media outlets and 675,000 institutional investors and brokers at their computer terminals. In addition, more than 14,300 journalists visit the PRN Press Room, an exclusive website for journalists to access real-time information and photos, and another 8,000 access global high-tech and healthcare releases from NEWSdesk International, PR Newswire's internet-based information retrieval and tracking company.

NEWSdesk gives you easy, highly customizable access to hundreds of news releases daily. Originally focused on technology, NEWSdesk now also carries releases in healthcare for companies, nonprofit organizations and agencies throughout the U.S. and around the world. NEWSdesk gives you news how you want it and when you want it, delivered straight to your desktop via its 'Breaking News' headlines e-mail service (also available on the web). And its 'Personal News' feature lets you set up news filters for specific topics of interest to you from 88 themes from the high-tech and healthcare world.

ProfNet, NEWSdesk's sister resource, is a collaborative of 10,000 public relations professionals linked by the internet and provides journalists and authors ready access to expert sources. ProfNet is "a direct link to 10,000 news and information officers at colleges and universities, corporations, think tanks, national labs, medical centers, nonprofits, and PR agencies." It serves as "a central collection-and-distribution point for reporters' queries and assists on hundreds of media projects weekly." With ProfNet, writers can locate sources both by sending queries via e-mail to segmented lists of PR officers (ProfNet Search) and also by searching a database of 2,700 prospective contacts (ProfNet's Experts Database).

With all these up-to-the-minute resources, your research will be a pleasure, your sources will be outstanding, and your editors will be pleased.

Knowing When Enough Is Enough

As you select and sort and organize your materials to answer the who, what, when, where, why, and how of the matters of concern to you and feel a sense of richness in all that you have gathered, you will know that you have researched enough. Most often, you will have found far more materials than you possibly can use for your assignment. If some category of your article is a bit thin, though, you can boost it with more research or a few more phone calls.

Being Complete

You will know that your research is complete and that your work is finished when you fit all your puzzle pieces together into your article.

- Does your article say what you had intended?
- Does it inform?
- Does it entertain?
- Does it inspire?
- Does it touch a nerve?
- Does it haunt you as you go about your day?
- Will it linger in the minds of your readers, too?

If a large base of readers can relate to what you have written, your research and authenticity will serve you well, and your readership will continue to grow. Next time your research will be even easier. You will know when to stop your current project so that you can begin your next exciting adventure in researching and writing.

Being Prepared Yet Staying Flexible While Interviewing

A few days after arranging an appointment for a telephone interview, I often post or e-mail a few questions that I plan to cover to the prospective interviewee. This thoughtful approach serves as a friendly reminder of the planned interview, helps the interviewee prepare a bit, helps attune the individual to your goal, and helps to put the interviewee at ease.

To put yourself at ease before an important interview, you may want to practice with an articulate friend. As you practice, note your friend's responses. Your friend also may choose to startle you with some answers to give you practice in maintaining your focus. After you complete your practice interview, think about the following questions.

- Were you well prepared to conduct your interview?
- Were your questions succinct?
- Were your questions clear?
- Were your questions too wordy?
- Did you talk too much?
- Did you give your interviewee ample time to speak?
- Were you listening closely?

- Did you rush in too soon with your next prepared question?
- Were you flexible so that you could follow up on important unanticipated aspects that your interviewee introduced?
- Were you quiet at the right moments?
- Did you avoid asking questions that could be answered merely with a yes or no?
- When you did not get the answer you wanted, did you come back to it later and ask it in a different way that was clearer to your interviewee? If so, what do you feel blurred the first version of your question?
- Were you persistent without being pushy or overbearing?
- Were you able to extract exciting quotes to spice up your article?
- Were you able to focus on the aspect of your article that you chose to develop?
- Did you maintain control of the interview?
- At the end of the interview, did you offer time for your interviewee to speak about something of interest that you perhaps had overlooked asking?

Taping or Not Taping

Some interviewers prefer not to tape. They find transcribing too time-consuming. Some find it useful to transcribe just the direct quotes that they plan to use. It is quick and easy with a tape recorder that has a working counter.

It is important also to keep your notes meticulously separated from the words of your sources and to give careful attribution for what interviewees share. Remember, in your final article you also can paint an image of the interviewee's surroundings from your jotted description to give more atmosphere to your piece.

Confirming Information

Many writers call back to double check the accuracy of information with interviewees. Some writers, because of deadline restrictions, may not have such a luxury. If you tape your interviews—with the permission of the interviewee—you can recheck their quotes and detailed statistics, facts, and other information quickly and conveniently. The service of a tape recorder in topnotch working condition cannot be overestimated. Tape recorders save you time and effort beyond measure. Remember always to make sure that you have new batteries for your tape recorder and that it is working well.

During the interview, be sure to give an occasional glance to check to make sure that your tape recorder is recording satisfactorily. Do this subtly, without distracting your interviewee. In addition, take some pertinent notes by hand just in case your tape recorder has a mechanical problem. You do not want to spend your time and the interviewee's time only to go away with fleeting memories of carefully chosen prose, a blank tape, and no notes.

It also is important to get the full name of your interviewee, his official professional title, his age (if appropriate), and his location on tape. Clarify the spelling of your interviewee's name, title, and location. Your accurate reporting protects your reputation. One of the best ways to support your accuracy is to use a tape recorder.

Joseph Sherman, an Associate Professor in the Department of English at the University of the Witwatersrand, Johannesburg, South Africa, and former Editor of *Jewish Affairs*, believes that "A tape recorder always should be used for interviews. . . . These tapes should be housed in a library or archive, for they are the proof that what finally is published is accurate, historical, and archival material." Sherman goes on to say, "The edited transcript of the interview as it is to be published—which may involve the reorganizing of points made later but which relate to an earlier question—always should be sent to the interviewee for final approval."

Sherman also explains, "It should be stressed to an interviewee that the discussion which takes place in oral form will not be published verbatim—often this would be repetitive and boring to a reader—but that it will be an edited, organized, and polished version that will retain entirely the idiom and words of the interviewee. Almost all those I have interviewed have appreciated this greatly."

Recently, I met a Brazilian professor who appreciates the approach that Sherman outlines. He told me, in fact, that he grants interviews only with writers who allow him to see the portions of their final transcripts in which his words appear. Because his scientific reputation is at stake, he guards his words and makes sure that he has been quoted accurately and interpreted correctly.

I believe in creating a climate of respect and camaraderie with interviewees. Similarly, Sherman says to keep the atmosphere of an interview as relaxed as possible. Even if you feel personal antagonism toward the topic, you must, as a good interviewer, "allow the discussant's ideas to come naturally without force-feeding or aggressiveness."

Meeting Your Deadline

Meeting your deadline with your editor is of utmost importance. This way all your material will be confirmed and approved, and you will have your well-written typescript on the editor's desk in time. Editors will be pleased when their checkers verify your data and confirm your quotes with your interviewees and find that you have done your work with super diligence.

Being Gracious

Always remember to send a note to thank your interviewees. Courtesy pays. Show respect to establish a fine working relationship, and the interviewee even may welcome contributing to some of your future articles. When your article is published, remember to send a complimentary copy to each of your interviewees with your words of thanks. Your interviewees will long remember. Some even may frame your work and display it in their offices.

Getting Model Releases

If you use photographs, remember to get model releases. Keep in mind that release forms for subjects appearing in photographs to be published in magazines vary widely. While there are certain criteria common to most release forms, they vary considerably in format and style from publisher to publisher. It will be most useful to deal directly with each publisher and follow precisely what each requires for best results.

Anthony Mark Dalessandro, former Communications Director, Order Sons of Italy in America, Washington, D.C., says, "As long as the names and photographs are used for news or informational purposes (not for promotional purposes), there is absolutely no need to get release forms. Of course libel and slander laws still apply."

Greg Jones, the Editor of *Sailing* Magazine, whom you first met in Chapter 2, "Getting on the Right Track," explains that when you submit a photograph of a recognizable person that will be used for advertising or commercial purposes, you should have the subject sign a model release form. To protect yourself, you will need a model release if you plan to use the photographs for something more than editorial purposes. You can use the forms provided by your editor.

Jones also says that you always should identify yourself as a member of the press and inform your subjects that you are dealing with them in your professional capacity. By continuing to cooperate with you, they give de facto (actual, even if not strictly legal) permission.

On the contrary, Jones points out that when the participant is involved in a newsworthy event or is a member of a crowd in a public place—and is not "singled out for special attention," then no model release in required. He is quick to add that the operative word here is "newsworthy" and goes on to say that "If, for example, the photograph relies upon the subject being portrayed in an embarrassing or compromising situation for its newsworthiness, then the photographer/publication could be liable for damages."

Jones says, "These are the bare bones concerning model releases. In practice, there are many variations. I have worked on small American news-papers where we required model releases for all minor children whose pic-tures were used in the newspaper. I have worked for magazines in the Middle East where we didn't publish pictures of anyone except adult males and for magazines in England where model releases were virtually never used, re-gardless of the subject."

Two points are clear: (1) Protect yourself, and, (2) find out what your publisher's and editor's policy is regarding model release forms.

Doing Your Homework

Before I interviewed Ron Franscell about his first novel, I read and stud-ied every word of *Angel Fire* so that I could ask—I hoped—thought-provok-ing and compelling questions. I also read what his publisher was saying about him, what readers were saying about his newspaper, *News-Record,* and his novel. In addition, I read other interviews he had done to prevent duplicating any questions that he had been asked interminably. As a result, he later said, ". . . your questions are the best I've fielded. They show insight and thought." Had I not done my homework, he probably would not have had those thoughts about my questions.

Similarly, years ago, before I interviewed the late Linus Pauling, double Nobel laureate, and the late Roger J. Williams, the discoverer of pantothenic acid and the "Father of Nutrition," I read their works avidly, read about them, and attended some of their public lectures. I had the great joy of many private conversations with Williams. Both he and Pauling appreciated my focused efforts to convey their messages with care.

Make interviewing as hassle-free as possible by doing your homework on your topic and your interviewee, if applicable. Know the slant for your article or articles—if you plan to use the same expert for more that one story. Ask succinct questions that focus on helping you to prepare articles that will be rejection-resistant. Happy interviewing!

• • •

Chapter 9.
Improving Your Style

Greg Jones of *Sailing* Magazine, who explained about model release forms in Chapter 8, says that "If your article is so well-written the editor can't stop reading it, it will be published. Guaranteed."

So how do you learn to write so well that the editor can't put it down? Jones shares what he calls "generic advice to any would-be writer."

> Read all the time. Read the best writers. Read as wide a variety of material as you can understand, and then some. Push your horizons. Attain a passing familiarity with as many disciplines as possible. Read the classics—everything from the *King James Bible* to Shakespeare to Conrad to Dostoyevsky—to more modern writers who may or may not become classics, people like Bill Bryson and John McPhee and Graham Greene. The list goes on and on. Just read. If you are to be a writer, then you also must be a reader.

Bob Powers, daily columnist for *The Marietta Times* and contributor to five websites, similarly says,

> Writers must read in every spare moment, not just for information or entertainment, but to assess how the great ones write. Read good newspapers. Haunt the closest library and read as many classics as possible. Dissect books to see how the author created the effects that worked to entrance millions of readers.

Liz Carpenter, author, lecturer, and equal rights leader, shares, "In my White House days, *To Kill a Mocking Bird* had just burst forth. Author Harper Lee came to a reception and advised would-be writers simply: 'Read your head off.'"

Think of it. When you read and look up the definitions of words new to you, you empower yourself with a wealth of knowledge and a key to the world—its past, its present, and its future. You travel beyond our galaxy. You peer inside the molecule, the atom, and the hadron. You are enlightened by multiple viewpoints and are privy to manyfold pathways of thinking. You experience a profusion of lifetimes vicariously.

Practicing Your Craft

Armed with your insatiable curiosity, your imagination, your wealth of knowledge and thoughts, color and ambience, texture and feel, you brim with stories to tell, predictions to make, and solutions to offer. You can entertain; you can inform; you can lead; you can make a difference when you practice your craft. Writing is your passion. Being published to share your ideas is your goal. Finding editors who share your vision is your mission.

Opportunities to practice your writing skills and to improve your style abound beyond your solitary world of labor and silent practice. You may choose to join small critique groups or attend writing workshops on site or take advantage of online writing workshops in your special field or fields of interest.

Maintaining High Standards

Introduce your articles with compelling hooks. Report facts with care.

When materials are open to interpretation, collect information from all sides, then analyze and present your view as objectively as you can.

If you have the luxury of finishing ahead of deadline, put away your typescript for a few days. Return to it with fresh new eyes. Then read your work as its editor.

Self-Editing Your Nonfiction

Ask yourself the following questions.

Regarding Your Introduction

- Is your introduction captivating enough to keep your readers reading?
- Do you get right to the point then guide your reader quickly down a well-marked path?
- What is the purpose of your article?
- Why is your material important?
- Why are you the best person to write this article?

Regarding Your Composition

- Is your article organized and developed in a logical order?

- Are steps missing that the reader needs in order to understand your information?
- Do you stay true to your goal, or do you wander off course, losing your bewildered reader who flips to the next article or tosses the magazine?
- Do you include information that intrigues you but does not fit in properly with the remaining material? If so, as difficult as it may seem, you must get rid of excesses.
- Do bullets or numbers help you to enumerate your story's salient presentation?
- Do you choose words that have the best tone for your subject matter?
- Do you employ vigorous verbs in active voice?
- Do you maintain a consistent verb tense?
- Do you use too many adjectives, or do you follow Mark Twain's advice in *Pudd'nhead Wilson*, "As to Adjectives: when in doubt, strike it out"?
- Will your words be understood easily by their intended audience?
- Are your sentences of varied lengths to prevent a choppy read?
- Are your sentences so long they cannot be read in one breath?
- Do your sentences have a pleasant rhythm? Read your article aloud and listen to its words and their cadence. Have you chosen powerful and melodious words?
- Do you give specific details that engage the senses of your readers and make your piece memorable from well-drawn images?

Have someone read your work aloud to you. Close your eyes and listen.

- In your mind's eye, as you listen, do your words show bursts of crimson and azure?
- Do you smell the fragrance of magnolias or the aroma of fresh baked brioche?
- Do you hear the lonesome moan of the midnight train?
- Must you dodge windswept leaves?
- Do you feel the chill from the blast of a sudden cold front?
- Are your sentences drab and flat?

Regarding Your Conclusion

- Will your conclusion linger in the minds of your readers, or is it merely a rehash of what you already have offered?

You will find additional questions to ponder in Chapter 12, "Controlling Your Inner Editor."

Deciding about Workshops—On Site and Online

You must decide for yourself whether workshops will work for you. Australian author Margaret McAlister, who often teaches workshops, says,

> Some are wonderful. Some are deadly dull, or repeat what you already know, or are full of people who are terribly serious about "writing as art." (That's fine if you are interested only in "literary" fiction, but if you want to write a commercial page-turner, it's not the best workshop for you.) Find out what's going to be taught, who's going to teach it, and whether you'll be doing exercises, working on your current writing project, or whatever. If you find the right writing workshop for you, it can change your life.

On the contrary, Professor Joseph Sherman, whom you first met in Chapter 8, says,

> I have never attended any writers' workshops. I have tried to learn from trial and error and the criticisms of others—editors, referees, and colleagues. In regard to the writing of fiction and poetry—something I personally do not do—I have, as an editor, found that work produced in a "writing workshop" tends to be contrived and artificial, following a set of "rules" laid down by the leader of the workshop and, therefore, often immediately identifiable. Such work, in the main, lacks spontaneity, freshness, and originality.

Many writers use workshops as springboards. Award-winning travel writer, Lynn Grisard Fullman, of Birmingham, Alabama, says, "When I was getting started, I attended several workshops and found them wonderful. It's great to be around other writers and editors to learn firsthand what editors want. I don't attend now. It's not that I couldn't learn more, but I think I need time to execute the wisdoms I've heard at these workshops. Beginners who want to attend should look for workshops involving editors. That's a great way to hear firsthand what a publication wants."

Finding Books Everywhere

You also will find your favorite libraries and bookstores teeming with everything from guides to grammar and instructions on basic writing skills to books on how to write a sonnet or a novel or how to hone your skills as a technical writer. The books are there waiting, but until you open them they may stay as a Chinese proverb says, " . . . but a block of paper."

Practicing to Achieve

Perhaps some of the information shared here will help to pave your way to a season of new growth and new writing adventures. With patience, persistence, and daily practice you will achieve your writing goals. If you write with joy and passion, you will spark joy and passion in others. When your writing ignites an interest in others to read, you are making a difference in your world. Happy practicing!

• • •

I'm writing in my head all my waking hours, it seems. Watching a TV sitcom, I will often rewrite the dialogue in my head. Reading a novel, even one I'm not going to review for a magazine, I find myself automatically critiquing it. When I attend a movie, I find myself thinking of good leads for a review.

Robert Powers
ANDOVER NEWS SERVICE
Greater Boston, MA

Chapter 10. Thinking It before You Write It

In writing classes and seminars, you often may hear that you must set pen to paper, crank a blank sheet of paper into your typewriter, or position your fingers over the keyboard of your computer and begin to write if you ever expect to see your finished story or article. That is true. During the process of writing, the story manifests, grows, and changes. But some instructors have said adamantly that you cannot write the piece in your head and then "release" it onto paper or into your computer. Those instructors believe that you must write your story for it to exist, much like an artist must paint a portrait before others can see it.

While I agree that you must settle down and write to produce a piece, the "you-can't-write-it-in-your-head" idea should be tossed straightaway. If people and projects prevent you from getting to your computer or even keep you from pulling out a wrinkled legal pad to begin that story or article you feel compelled to write, writing in your head rises as a most welcome and viable choice. When I was planning to write a fitness article—"Maintaining Muscle Mass"— I had read from source after source and had found an abundance of material, but constant interferences made it impossible to write the article.

Enduring Countless Interruptions

Like everyone else I know, I was riding an ever-moving merry-go-round of time-consuming tasks. First, I was busy with meetings and dinner parties. I had to do interviews and photo shoots. Then there was a Friday night telephone call from a New York editor who wanted me to write an article and send it to him by FedEx the following Monday. I also had to tie up loose ends on household repairs, then shop and pack for an upcoming holiday trip.

"Pre-Writing" on a Subconscious Level

Nevertheless, I worked on the article on a subconscious level. Also, between scores of everyday activities, my thoughts would ease away and embrace the fitness article like a would-be lover.

While I relished the refreshing change of scene and reveled in the fun, on another level, even flying, swimming, playing tennis, and horseback riding were intrusive.

At last, while others shrieked and shielded their eyes from a sandstorm, I dashed to the safety of our vacation suite; and in the darkness and silence of a 45-minute power outage, I used my trusty Eveready flashlight in its lantern form to light my way to outline on paper the focus of my article.

Waiting for the Perfect Time to Write?

If you wait until everything is perfect to settle down to write your story or article, you probably never will write it. In that case, the instructors alluded to earlier are correct. If you contemplate your topic, meditate on it, and write your article in your head, procrastination never can reign. Writer's block never will divorce you from your thoughts. In fact, you will be feverish to write down your thoughts. You will take the reins and proceed through errands and friends and chaos and work and chores and hobbies and holiday fun and just write.

So toss that old myth that you cannot write until you start putting your words down on paper or keystroking them. It is not only okay to write in your head for a terrific head start, sometimes it is a must. The wait also can allow your subconscious mind to work through the materials to help you produce an even finer work when you do manage the time to write.

Similarly, Bob Powers, who writes book and music reviews for newspapers and websites, including the *Web Magazine, G21: The World's Magazine*, says:

> I'm writing in my head all my waking hours, it seems. Watching a TV sitcom, I will often rewrite the dialogue in my head. Reading a novel, even one I'm not going to review for a magazine, I find myself automatically critiquing it. When I attend a movie, I find myself thinking of good leads for a review.

Writing, At Last

Finally, I created the time to write. On the next two mornings, I crept out around 5:00 a.m. to write at the poolside. I sat silently and wrote on a legal pad. After having allowed my subconscious and conscious thoughts to ripen, the article flowed right out of my head, down my arm, and through my pen onto the paper with notable ease. Later, I was able to keystroke the article into my Mac then polish the work and make sure that I had adhered to the editor's word limit before finally submitting it. Even when articles seem to flow to you, remember the all-important polishing before submitting your final work. You will read more about this crucial aspect in Chapter 17, "Cooperating with Editors."

• • •

Chapter 11.
Writing Warmups

It is commonly accepted that

> Jumping from little or no exercise into a fitness program that would make a professional athlete pant can cause injury and can destroy the best intentions about getting fit. With proper encouragement and gradual involvement, countless exercise enthusiasts would stay dedicated.... Warmups prepare the mind and the body for exercise.
>
> *Balance Fitness*
> May 1996

Thus, warmups are instrumental in helping to establish the habit of exercising. Could writing warmups prepare the mind and body for writing? Could writing warmups be crucial in helping to establish the habit of writing daily in a dedicated place at a designated time?

Let Your Inner Editor Take a Holiday

When you do your writing warmups, let your "inner editor" take a holiday. You will discover more about this "holiday" in honor of the inner editor in the next chapter. During warmups, do not worry about organization or transitions or finding the best word. Just write. Do not edit. Use whatever works well for you. If you feel more comfortable handwriting your first drafts, do so. If you feel more at ease composing straight into your computer, do so. If you are afraid that you may forget some of your thoughts, you may choose to preserve them on a tape recorder to refer to later.

At first when you write freely without editing, you may be prone to use fantastic adjectives and stately adverbs to perpetuate your passage, and your descriptions may be too long by today's standards. Nevertheless, you are writing. You can observe your descriptions evolve over time. More and more, you will rely on active high action verbs to invigorate your passages. Later, you will interweave description smoothly into the action or characters or incident or setting to move the plot of a story. You will build the who, what, why, when, where, and how of the story or article.

A Few Writing Warmups to Try

Writing Descriptions

To get your writing muscles wakened and warmed, you can begin by describing something as simple as the chilled orange juice and no-sugar added shredded wheat you had for breakfast this morning. Or you could describe the mellow coffee and stack of homemade blueberry pancakes drizzled with hot maple syrup and real creamery butter that you savored.

Writing Comparisons and Contrasts

As a beginning warmup, you can compare and contrast the foods you ate as a youngster with the foods you eat now or the sports you played in your youth with the sports you play now. You can write about the books you reveled in as a child and compare and contrast them to the books you enjoy now. The possibilities for this exercise are endless.

Adding Setting

You can write as many sentences, paragraphs, or pages as you wish. If you choose, you can interweave setting into your description. You can write about the white stone tables sheltered by huge blue umbrellas where you nibbled a croissant. You can describe the bright red booths at the diner where you devoured ham and eggs. Or you can describe the sticky sidewalk where you stood and gulped a cup of hot black coffee and gobbled a chocolate-covered donut at a street vendor's place while you waited for AAA to tow your car and its ailing fan belt. You get the idea. Break away from rules for the moment. Free yourself to write. Exceed standard word limits for sentences. Write. Embellish. Develop. You can correct, smooth, and polish later.

Describing What's in the Box?

This practice requires a "concealer" and a "listener." Have your concealer place an item in a small box or opaque bag and close it without allowing either you or the listener to see the item. Open the box or bag just enough to reach inside to study the item only by touch for a minute or two.

Write your description of the physical characteristics—dimensions, shape, texture, weight, and aroma and even sound, if any—without giving away too quickly what the item is.

Next, write your description of the item in terms of essence and what it possibly could symbolize, but remember to maintain suspense as you describe it. Leave the clichés sleeping and reach for descriptive terms, phrases, and comparisons that are yours alone. The goals are to articulate with accuracy and brevity yet to engage the reader's eager anticipation for your final words and to convey successfully what the item is.

Amusing, Enlightening, and Touching the Reader

Now read your descriptions to a friend who was not privy to the contents. Watch the expression on the face of your listener. Is the listener amused, enlightened, or touched by your descriptions? Do you engage interest and, at the same time, convey the identity of the item?

Writing from the Viewpoint of an Inanimate Object

You also can describe the item in the box from its viewpoint. Free your imagination to explore different dimensions either solemnly or humorously. Try both. You can describe what it must be like to be a paper clip. Does the paper clip's status matter to it? Is it glad to be holding together two important documents on the desk of the president of one of the finest universities in the world? Does it hurt to be squashed in a file with 23 other documents, all with other paper clips, and slammed into a cold dark filing cabinet away from friendly smiles and the warm touch of human hands for days or sometimes weeks? Does it enjoy traveling by airmail from country to country? Did it ever slide onto the wrong document and travel to the wrong office in some faraway land where all other paper clips were foreign to it? How many times has it been stepped on or had coffee spilled on it? Free your imagination and write.

Writing about Memories Stirred from Aromas and Fragrances

Sit quietly with your favorite kitchen spices and herbs before you. With your eyes closed, waft the aromas, one at a time, and savor each scent. When one especially stirs your emotions and fires up old memories, do not identify the scent or intellectualize about it. Simply luxuriate in the feelings that the fragrance evokes and immediately write down those feelings. From those feelings written as a warmup, you sometimes can create full-blown stories or articles.

When you smell an herb such as sage, can you practically see your grandmother in her cozy kitchen lifting a golden-brown turkey from the oven, setting the pan carefully on wrought iron trivets, then sliding a cookie sheet covered with homemade rolls into that overworked oven? Smell and write.

Similarly, when you smell your favorite perfumes or colognes or incense or essential oils what memories do they stir? What feelings do they evoke? Write what you feel.

Writing about Sounds

Sit quietly in a favorite room or in a forest or at the beach with your eyes closed. Listen to the sounds around you. Study them. Determine their sources. How quiet is your world? Which sounds stir you emotionally? Which sounds are nurturing? Which sounds would you miss most? Which are upsetting? After listening for 15 to 20 minutes, write about the sounds you heard. Describe how they made you feel and what they made you remember. Have these sounds triggered an idea for a story or an article?

Using Multi-purpose Writing Exercises

When your memories take you back to your childhood, you also can pick a single event and use it as a warmup. Not only writing classes use this exercise, but also some self-improvement courses use such practices to help adults get in touch with frozen feelings. After you write your own feelings about an incident, you may want to write about those feelings from the possible viewpoint of another person who observed the same incident in the past. If you are able to do this, you may gain great insight to help yourself not only in your writing but also in your ongoing, growing relationship with yourself as a person. Your exploration may bring great rewards.

Other writing warmup exercises that help you to explore this important relationship involve writing with brutal honesty about your likes and dislikes. You can write about everything from pastas to policies to people. What and whom do you appreciate? What and whom can you hardly tolerate? After your writing warmup practice and potential catharsis, you can shred the writing, if you choose.

Or with identities changed, incidents manipulated, and plot magnified, perhaps you can develop what began as a mere warmup or self-improvement practice into a bestselling novel or a nonfiction work to expose a problem and offer viable solutions to help others. You can use your talent to write about a cause of concern to you.

Completing an Article

When you find a story or an article in a newspaper, magazine, or book that intrigues you, read the first paragraph, then stop. Go to your computer, or pull out a legal pad and compose what you believe could flow logically from the material that you just read. Do this frequently. Then compare what you have written with what was published. Was your organization better than that of the original article? Were you transitions smoother? Was your piece more succinct? Relish that your writing is enjoyable to readers, too.

Warming Up for Success

Remember, writing warmups can help you to thaw and express your inner feelings. They can help you to establish a place and time to write. With enough practice, they will help you to create the habit of writing daily. They can help you to stay disciplined so that you can accomplish your writing goals. Even after you graduate to full-blown writing projects and assignments, you may find that writing warmups are one of your best friends when you feel that your writing is stiff and cold. Take a few minutes and use your imagination to turn your project or assignment into a writing warmup, and soon your writing may sizzle; and you will be on your way to a successful finish. Happy workout!

• • •

....No matter how good a story may be, we cannot afford to waste our time sludging through errors and will simply send it back. Be professional. Editors are not your enemies, but we do not operate on charity.

Guy Lancaster
THE ARKANSAS REVIEW
Jonesboro, AR

An otherwise salable article on a fascinating topic could be doomed by errors, which make the potential buyer wary of the entire product's integrity, not just the poorly written portions.

Julia Bencomo Lobaco
VISTA
Coral Gables, FL

Not sticking to the word counts is the most glaring faux pas writers make. When we say no more than 1,400 words for a feature, including sidebar, that's what we mean! It's amazing how many writers send us 3,000-, or even 4,000-word, stories then expect us to edit them to fit our format.

Gena Holle
INTERNATIONAL RAILWAY TRAVELER
San Diego, CA

Chapter 12.
Controlling Your Inner Editor

Appreciating the Grand View

In his book, *Rethinking Education*, the late Roger J. Williams, Ph.D., world-renowned scientist and educator wrote,

> It is conceivable that an extremely myopic individual might spend a lifetime studying the Grand Canyon of the Colorado inch by inch and fail utterly to see its grandeur. Likewise, educators and scholars who are extreme specialists are myopic and may never see the 'grand view' of world knowledge as a whole. We too often encourage students to study world knowledge bit by bit without ever appreciating that it all fits together.

Composing before You Cut and Change

Similarly, when you don't force your "inner editor"—that editor-in-your mind—to take a holiday when you are writing warmups or stories or articles or books, you may never see the whole work and how it all fits together. That eager editor will peruse and pick at every letter, every word, every sentence, and every paragraph. Your inner editor will add, rearrange, and scratch out entire pages. Your story, article, or book will start to develop, then parts—and potentially all—of it will be swept away like the sand beneath your feet in the rushing tide at the beach. Beginning to write, then interrupting to inspect, to evaluate, and to rewrite line by line can destroy a work.

In *Portraits from Memory*, Bertrand Russell describes this problem: "When I was young, each fresh piece of serious work used to seem to me for a time—perhaps a long time—to go beyond my powers. I would fret that it was never going to come right. I would make one unsatisfying attempt after another, and in the end have to discard them all...."

Finishing the Piece, Then Putting It on Hold

You first must allow your imagination to team up with your writing skills to produce a piece. If the word length of your story or article is within a range that you can accomplish during an allotted writing session and you have the time to write a complete rough draft of your article or story from start to finish in one sitting, it is a great advantage to the fine development of your work. Just write, write, write. Do not edit. If your deadline permits, it also will serve you well to put your typescript away for a few days to cool your passion for it.

Finally Inviting Your Inner Editor to Edit

When you return to read your work, then you must welcome "that editor-in-your-mind" home from the holiday and invite your inner editor to edit. Now that you have written without evaluating or attacking your work and have distanced yourself from your work by putting it on hold for a few days, you have greater objectivity, and you can read it with greater clarity.

Now you must disown your work for the moment and thoughtfully rid it of as many flaws as you can. With each reading, edit for a different potential error. During your first editing session, you may choose to pay extra close attention to your spelling. Do not rely on a spell checker. Use your spell checker only after you have read for meaning and completed your own inspection. If you hastily type "to" even though you certainly meant to type "too," your super handy, ever-diligent spell checker cannot know your intention, and it will not warn you of your error. Next, you may decide to proofread for subject—verb agreement errors. On your third reading, you may search for punctuation errors. Make sure that you have carefully composed each sentence. While some editors may allow fragments, run-on sentences, and comma splices for special effect, many editors abhor such constructions. Also, you will want to proofread your work and pay close attention to transitions. Look for repetitions. Search out passive voice and replace it with active voice. Replace weak verbs with vigorous verbs. Make sure that you are maintaining a consistent verb tense. Read your work aloud and listen to its rhythm and rich sounds.

Think of ridding the flaws from your typescript as a carnival duck shoot. Bag as many ducks as you can and take home a teddy bear. In the case of your story or article, if you polish your piece well enough, you will win publication and a check from the editor of your target anthology or magazine. If you have the luxury of time on your side, put your work away for a day or two, then take it out and read it as objectively as you can. Trim and polish more, if needed.

Editing Your Own Work

In General—Ask Yourself

- Does the title titillate its readers?
- Is the title suitable to the work and to its target market?

- Does your opening sentence entice the reader and hold attention?

About Your Story—Ask Yourself

- Is your story the right genre for your target market?
- Will enough readers relate to your story to want to read it, or is its theme too specialized?
- Does the story develop in a believable fashion?
- Does the theme of your story build logically?
- Does your chain of incidents link together in the most powerful order?
- Is your setting clear?
- Is the immediacy or time limit of your story short enough to make and keep the story suspenseful?
- Does the plot of your story unfold dramatically and hold the reader's attention?
- Do you keep your story flowing with the just right details?

Robert J. Sawyer, author of a dozen science fiction novels and winner of the Nebula Award and 20 other national and international writing awards, says, "Often I draft whole scenes simply as dialogue, without speech attribution tags (no "I said," "he said," "Bob said"). That lets me focus entirely on what the scene is supposed to say. And once I do know exactly what it is I want to say, it's then easy to go back and add in appropriate descriptive details and even humorous asides that precisely underscore the point I'm trying to make. If you try to make up the details as you go along, you're just putting in window dressing, because you don't yet know what details would be appropriate."

- Are your characters well drawn?
- Can you feel each character's pain or joy?
- Do your characters speak with convincing dialogue?
- Are there sufficient conflicts and challenges for the protagonist to overcome?
- Do you have an endearing positive supporting character or characters and an unforgettable antagonist?
- Is the tone that you want in your story developed and maintained or changed as you desired?

- Does your story have a beginning, a middle, and an end?
- Does your story capture your reader's attention?
- Does your story impact the reader?
- Does your story linger in the mind of the reader?

Ron Franscell, the author of *Angel Fire,* says,

Writing is revising. Perhaps Kerouac needn't have revised, and that rawness became the beauty of his work. But the bulk of writing today, particularly for writers who yearn to be published, is a far more deliberate exercise.

In newspapering, being able to write a 'final' draft the first time is a much-vaunted talent. We don't often have time to revise as much as we should, and that's why journalism has often been called the 'first, rough-draft of history.' In the beginning, I deluded myself into thinking 20 years of newspapering had made me a genius at extemporaneous wordsmithing. How wrong I was. The beauty of *Angel Fire,* to me, is the simplicity wrought by agonizing over every word, repeatedly.

Don't fool yourself into thinking you've done it perfectly the first, fifth, or 50th time. I added a 'crucial' line to *Angel Fire* on the afternoon the publisher shipped it to the printer! Today when I drift across words in my book, I often think of better words. Revision frees you, a little, from a lifetime of second-guessing. But I will also say this: There comes a time to let go. You cannot revise forever and hope to see your work in print. Let your writing's flaws be called 'style' by critics and get on to the next story.

About Your Article—Ask Yourself
Introduction
- Will your opening sentence intrigue your readers?
- Do you stay on your topic or wander away and lose your reader?
- Is your slant appropriate for your target market?
- Are there sufficient eager readers who want to learn about your topic?
- Is the sale of your article supported by a market willing to purchase the magazine?
- Do you set your intended tone early?

Composition
- Can you meet your readers' needs with a suitable breadth and depth of information?

- Do you offer enough new and useful information to merit publication?
- Are your points organized in a meaningful order so that your work flows?
- Are your points well substantiated?
- Is your message sharply focused, or do you wander and add extraneous information that is enchanting to you but is intrusive in this particular article?
- Do you use too many words to make your points?
- Do you use the best words to convey your meaning?
- Do you use active voice?
- Do you use action verbs?
- Do you maintain verb tense?
- Do you paint a vivid image that your reader can see?
- Can your reader hear, feel, smell, and touch what you bring to life through your words?
- Are your words compelling?
- Do you convey your message in a way that entices the reader to keep reading?
- Do you mesmerize your reader?
- Can you tighten up some sentences and delete some others to improve the readability of your article?
- Are any sentences scattered that should be brought together for greater clarity?
- Are repetitious sentences marring your article? If so, you can delete the ones that are ineffective or modify both and weave them together for finer detail.
- Can you rearrange a paragraph here and there to smooth the flow of your piece?
- Are your transitions smooth?
- Are anecdotes used in other articles in your target magazine? If so, can you use anecdotes to help convey your message?
- Do you give useful examples and extrapolations to guide your readers?
- Do you have quotes from authorities on both sides of the issue you are explaining?
- Have you met or exceeded your editor's word limit for your article?
- Have you successfully conveyed the who, what, when, where, why, and how about your topic?

Conclusion

- Does your conclusion wrap up your article well?
- Have you acknowledged your sources either in the text or as footnotes or following the body of your text, according to your editor's preference?
- Have you noted personal communication sources following the text?
- Do you maintain the tone that you set out to create in your piece?
- Does your tone change as you intended?
- Finally, ask yourself, have you entertained, surprised, astonished, or informed your reader with the information in your article?

Recognizing the Proper Time and Place

Editing is important, but there is a time and place for it. It must not come too soon. Editing too soon is like weeding a garden before the tender sprouts of its new plants are distinguishable from young weeds in freshly turned soil. Good plants can be killed with ill-timed weeding. Good stories, articles, and books can be destroyed with ill-timed editing. When the garden is established—when the pea plants are clearly pea plants and corn plants are clearly corn plants—then the weeding can be done to the betterment of the entire garden.

Likewise, you must allow yourself to develop your story or article to see its overall "landscape" before you begin to evaluate, eliminate, or rearrange material. The more you are able to do this, the better your stories and articles will be in their final polished forms. Given time to warmup, time to write, time to cool down, and distance to gain clarity before editing, the grander the view of your final work will be. Happy editing!

• • •

Chapter 13. Grabbing an Editor's Attention

You're all set to go out for grilled sirloin. Just anticipating the delicious meal you are about to enjoy makes your mouth water. How would you like it if the server delivered a charred chunk of meat to your table instead? Or what if you are a vegetarian, but your date insists on taking you out for steak? If you live and breathe Beethoven and your ears curl over at the lonesome sounds of Willie Nelson, what do you do when friends keep giving you Willie Nelson CDs?

Similarly, when you pitch a query to an editor, make sure it is prepared precisely to suit his needs and tastes. If an editor says that he needs articles on the koala, Australia's "arboreal ambassador," as the koala has been called, then don't query the editor about black bears; and don't send him an article about teddy bears.

If your target magazine has articles on "Acupuncture for Your Allergies," "Bach Flower Remedies for Your Mood Swings," and "Naturopathic Care for Your Tots," then probably you would not do well to submit a query about laser surgery.

If your target journal touts the promise of a tiny selenium-saturated sponge as a breakthrough in glaucoma treatment, then probably it is not wise to submit a query on "The Role of Nutrition in Glaucoma Prevention."

On the other hand, if the editor telephones to request that you prepare an article on "A Surgical Breakthrough in Glaucoma Treatment," you can compose the article exactly as the editor has explained that he wants it. Then, if you choose, when you submit your completed typescript, you can include a sidebar such as "Nutrition for Healthy Eyes," just in case he might like to use it to round out the article.

Recognizing Likes and Dislikes

Often the likes and dislikes of editors are blatant. Look at food magazines. The distinction between the various food publications used to be more obvious than it is now. Some recipes practically dripped drizzled butter from their pages and titillated your taste buds with cups of sugar. Some other magazines presented recipes using vegetable oils and honey, instead. Notice the inclusion of other ingredients such as miso, tofu, tempeh, soymilk, wakame, and sea salt. While some of these ingredients may be called for in a mainstream food magazine recipe, they are more likely to be included among the ingredients for natural recipes often referred to as "health foods." Some of these magazines even present recipes suitable for allergy sufferers, for they sometimes use no wheat, no milk, and no eggs.

The trend with many magazine recipes now is to go lighter on fats and sugar. Still it is fairly easy to discern what type of food and recipe-related article to pitch if you study several issues of your target magazine. Study their competitors, too, to see for yourself just what the differences are and what may be approaching. If you can anticipate trends, you certainly can please your editor.

Intrigue an editor by surprising her with just what she would like to receive. Always avoid the temptation to try to be "original" with gimmicks, strange letterheads, gaudy colored paper, weird fonts, odd punctuation, or unusual spelling.

Presenting a Professional Package

Paul Grogan, Deputy Editor of *Global Adventure*, London, England, says, "It's all about presenting a professional package. Know your target magazine inside out. Only then can you hope to have any idea about what the editor is after. Then you can present a choice of original story ideas in clear, concise summaries, tailored to a specific section in a specific publication. Make it difficult for the editor to say no. If you were in his shoes, what would you want to see?"

G.W. Amick of Spain, whom you last met in Chapter 6, "Composing a Sparkling Query Letter," says, "Many times I can just look at the envelope and form an opinion. When I open the envelope, my opinion is justified. Just as I thought, no cover letter. You already know which basket that envelope went in. Yes, I like it; or no, I don't. The envelope, the paper, the presentation, the first paragraph must grab my attention. Of course the body of the story sells the story, not the first paragraph. . . ." In Chapter 14, "Balancing Your Communication," Amick will share his secret for excellent endings.

Showing Diligence

Karen Menehan, the Editor of *Massage Magazine*, Santa Cruz, California, says, "The most effective thing a writer can do to grab my attention is to tell me what sets her topic apart from others and why that topic will be of value to our readers. When a writer tells me clearly why her topic is new, unique, a trend, or supports our publication's mission of reflecting healthy touch in a positive light, it cuts down on the work I do to analyze the topic and promotes confidence on my part in the knowledge and sincerity of the writer."

You can appeal to M.J. Van Deventer, the Editor of *Persimmon Hill*, with an angle that is unusual, fresh, or unique. Once again, reflect on her advice shared in Chapter 2, "Getting on the Right Track," "It needs to be obvious that writers have studied my publication and our guidelines by adhering to the suggestions in the guidelines."

Similarly, Harold Ort, the Editor of *Popular Communications*, Hicksville, New York, says, "In a nutshell, know the topic you're writing about and our magazine. Visit the newsstand or ask for a complimentary copy, then familiarize yourself with the topics. If you've got a well-written article, grab my attention by going back to basics—including photos with captions and re-reading your article putting yourself in my shoes. Are there areas that beg for additional writing?"

Supplying Photos and Transparencies

Some publications are illustration-driven. Their editors only consider submissions which include B&W glossy photos, color photos, or color transparencies. If the photo does not practically tell your story on its own, neither your photos nor your article will win over the editor's heart.

Robert Joseph, the Editor of *Weekend Woodcrafts*, Concord, California, says, "I have found that 'a picture is worth a thousand words.' To grab my attention, show me what you can do, plain and simple. The picture can be something you made or a picture of a drawing that you plan on making. I need to know what you are going to build so that I can check my records to see if it has not been built yet and also to see if it fits into our editorial direction."

Wendy McCallum of *Healthy Options* says that interesting photographs and artwork that can be sourced and included help to boost the chance of article acceptance.

Some editors must see photos with all inquiries and submissions. Andy Sperandeo, the Editor of *Model Railroader*, Waukesha, Wisconsin, says, "To grab my attention a writer must include topnotch model railroad photography along with any inquiry or article submitted to us." He says that his contributors are generally hobbyists rather than professional writers, so that he and his staff are prepared to coach them and to rewrite their submissions if needed; because it is easier and less expensive than to have to replace their photography.

He explains that even professional photographers often have a hard time getting images his magazine can use. If you have both excellent writing and photographic skills, contemplate Sperandeo's words: "Because photography is such an important part of our magazine, and our subject matter is so challenging to photograph, a writer who can provide the closeup model photography we need will definitely get my attention."

Old House Interiors is "art-driven" and "showcases the best of today's period rooms, both historical and interpretive." The fine photography enchants readers and pulls them in to read the articles, so it is absolutely imperative that you know how your article should be illustrated. *Old-House Interiors* writer's guidelines advise you to send "scouting pictures with your proposal."

Some editors would like to see an enormous number of transparencies so that they can choose the very best to accompany your article. Grogan of *Global Adventure* says, "If you have hundreds of accompanying transparencies, so much the better."

Preparing Your Typescript

If you win that go-ahead to prepare a typescript, a few basics follow just in case they can help a bit.

The appearance of your typescript speaks for you when the rushed first reader picks it up from a huge stack of submissions. As you now have read in this book from numerous editors from around the world, if your submission is clean, crisp, and well-formatted, it will command greater respect. Having worked as an editor for many years, I can share with you that almost always "appearance perfect" typescripts also were well written. Writers who write well usually also pay attention to details and submit their typescripts with care.

Guy Lancaster of *The Arkansas Review* says, "Perhaps in a perfect world, editors would regard none of the mundane details and examine only the text to see whether or not it fits their needs, but that is not how things work. We want to publish good, solid stories and articles, but if something arrives with the ink smeared and several words misspelled, you have not given us a good first impression. I know that to many people, this sounds simply like common sense, and indeed, I thought the same before I took a seat on the other side of the editor's desk. Most of the stuff we receive has not been proofread for errors and is not printed neatly. No matter how good a story may be, we cannot afford to waste our time sludging through errors and will simply send it back. Be professional. Editors are not your enemies, but we do not operate on charity."

Persevering

When you get a response, if it is a rejection that comes months and months over the publisher's reported response time, what does that mean? Find a comrade who can suggest some questions to help you sort through the momentary disappointment.

- Does this mean the editor was almost interested?
- Does this mean that you were close to winning over the editor, but he already had a similar project in queue?

- Did the editor toy with your proposal "a few hours" or days during the many months while you waited?
- Did the editor perhaps sadly say, "No"?
- Does it mean that your work was in the slush pile until the week before you received the rejection?
- Did some overburdened mailroom person rip open the envelope, toss it in the general direction of the desk of a first reader or an editor?
- Did that editor give it a sidewise glance while reaching for those airline tickets to Tahiti then scrawl a note for the next person in the chain to send out a form rejection?
- Did the editor like your style and invite you to send other articles later?

Think through a whole host of possibilities. Then force a smile and try again. Remember, another editor is waiting to see your work.

Look at your work again, and ask yourself these questions.

- Will your lead intrigue your editor?
- Is your focus specific enough?
- Since the time of submitting your query, do you have new and better anecdotes to share for your proposed article?
- Can you arrange for an interview now that you could not when you first began investigating your topic?
- Do you need to edit and revise your work a bit more to make it desirable to your editor?

Being Encouraged

Above all, do not be discouraged by rejections. They are mere pieces of paper or sometimes simple e-mail messages. What is rejected today by one publisher may be loved by another one tomorrow. Self-improvement courses abound where their excellent teachers suggest, "Think of each rejection as simply part of the process that brings you one step closer to success." Be encouraged, be nurtured, and keep writing!

When it seems that no one is there for you, pick up this book, and read these words of encouragement again. Believe in yourself. Appreciate positive criticism, and be boosted by the improvements that can come from it. Avoid negative criticism whenever possible. But if it comes from some unfeeling person, keep your chin up and keep on working to improve your craft, and you can succeed.

As an aside, let me tell you about an experience of American romance novelist Fern Michaels. When asked, "How do you deal with rejection?" she said, "I'm happy to say I was never rejected. I absolutely find this amazing. I was at the right place at the right time and sold my first novel. However, at one point in time I wrote a letter to my, then, idol—Phyllis Whitney. I even had the audacity to send her a two-page sample of my work. She responded six months later and told me to forget about writing and to keep doing whatever it was I was doing, which was being a wife and a mother. I cried for days. I was too ashamed to tell anyone about her letter. Two years later, *Captive Passions* went on the New York Times Bestseller List and stayed on for six or seven weeks. I didn't write Ms. Whitney. I did think about it, though. Most writers read the list. If she didn't see it, that's okay too."

Fern went on to say, "I knew I had a thousand stories in me, not just one. What I didn't know was if I was good enough. She said, 'No.' I said, 'Yes.' I knew myself well enough to know that writing was what I wanted to do. I kept at it. Here I am. The words 'give up' are not in my vocabulary. Phyllis Whitney is not an editor. If an editor or several editors, told me there was no merit in my work, I think I might have given up. The keyword here is 'might.' Persevere and prevail."

It also may interest you to know that Fern now has published over 70 novels, and as a single mom, she put her five children "through college on [her] own with no help from anyone." In 1990, she established The Fern Michaels Foundation. She awards two full university scholarships annually to worthy students who otherwise would not be able to afford to attend a university. In addition, she has opened child care centers that offer reasonable rates to accommodate working single moms.

Continue to analyze your possible publications and their readers. Study, analyze, and practice your craft—whether you write fiction like Fern or nonfiction. Keep in mind the tremendous number of competitors. Do your best. Stay focused and keep trying. You can succeed.

Regarding Rejections

Joseph Sherman, who shared his opinion of workshops in Chapter 9, "Improving Your Style," also says not to be discouraged by rejections. He points out that the work of writing involves "a great deal of revision, and often several rewrites." He encourages you to maintain your own interest in what you are doing by putting away the rejected piece for a month or two and then returning to it with fresh eyes. He says, "Try to read what you have written with the eyes of the harshest critic. Show your writing to friends or colleagues whose judgement you respect, and on whom you can rely for honest appraisal, and keep on polishing and amending."

If an editor says she likes your writing but is not interested in your topic choice, then you obviously have the mechanics of writing under control, and that is important. Study additional issues of your target magazine, contemplate the advertisements more fully, re-read the writer's guidelines. Sometimes rejections still will come even with meticulous targeting.

If you receive a note from an editor who says he already has a story similar to yours in queue, then you know that you are on the right track. Let rejections motivate you simply to try again.

Remember also that some publishers have a three-month lead time. Some may have a six-month to a year or more lead time. Those with very brief lead times need very timely articles. Those with longer lead times are more likely to accept perennial articles.

Finding the just right publisher may be the writer's biggest challenge. If you believe that your writing skills are sharp and that your ability to gather data is topnotch, you may be encouraged to recall what Tim Horan, the editor of *The Greyhound Review,* said about "good writing" in Chapter 4, "Knowing Your Audience." To reiterate, Horan says, "It doesn't matter how good the writing is if it doesn't fit the audience." So study your abundant target publications with diligence. Attract your editor's attention with your keen understanding of his publication's audience and keep trying. You will succeed.

• • •

If your article is so well-written the editor can't stop reading it, it will be published. Guaranteed.

Greg Jones
SAILING
Port Washington, WI

It doesn't matter how good the writing is if it doesn't fit the audience.

Tim Horan
THE GREYHOUND REVIEW
Abilene, KS

To grab my attention a writer must include topnotch model railroad photography along with any inquiry or article submitted to us.

Andy Sperandeo
MODEL RAILROADER
Waukesha, WI

It's not about glitzy photos or illustrations or trying to impress an editor with facts. Attract your editor's attention by going back to basics and include photos *with* captions."

Harold Ort
POPULAR COMMUNICATIONS
Hicksville, NY

Chapter 14. Balancing Your Communication

One-sided arguments can irritate readers and cause them to flip the page to find a more objective article. In most cases, of course, the article never will reach print because a great many editors will reject such articles.

Keep in mind an idea of thinkers throughout the ages that is succinctly voiced by Bertrand Russell in *The Sceptical Essays*: "Even when the experts all agree, they may well be mistaken." Seek divergent opinions. Out-of-balance articles usually are guilty on any number of counts—attacking, overselling, and overtelling. Study the tone of the articles in your target publication, and ask yourself the following questions.

- Do the articles show divergent viewpoints from opposing experts?

- Do you feel confident to handle the material for your article objectively?

- Will you be able to show both sides of an issue in the allotted word limit?

- Can you supply materials from your own experience and from other resources and interviewees?

- Do the bulk of the articles rely on statements from authorities in their fields, or are the majority of the articles written by experts on their topics?

- What are the customs of the readers?

- What approximate age are the readers?

- What are the locations of the readership of your target magazine?

Your goal in nonfiction writing is to capture the attention of your readers, titillate their imaginations through the riveting and almost mystery-like development of your presentation, and leave them entertained, satisfied, and informed. First, though, whatever you plan to write—your feature idea or projected travel location or proposed personality profile and its unique slant or a how-to piece or new product report—you must win your editor's approval to line up an assignment. Find out if the publication has topics that are taboo. Never submit queries on an editor's taboo topics. Find the right editor for topics of interest to you.

Working to be Objective

Reading avidly from a wide variety of sources that espouse diverse political, social, philosophical, and spiritual views can help to broaden your scope. Reading different levels of presentations from complex scientific writings to garden-variety exposés and listening closely to the words people choose to speak in everything from formal speeches to over-the-fence chats with a friendly neighbor can help to enhance your ability to see multiple viewpoints and finally to find a balanced view.

Joseph Sherman, who offered some encouraging words regarding rejections in Chapter 13, explains, "Writers should balance factual information with human interest: how does what I am saying to my reader help him or her to identify with and relate to the information I am imparting? A lightness of touch in the style—irony, wit, and gentle good humor—always engages the interest and sympathy of a reader. Even a polemical piece, taking the strongest issue with another position, is made engaging by a style that seizes and maintains the interest of the reader. Style is all-important here: good journalistic writing is always logical in argument, organized in presentation of data, and communicates with wit or with elegance."

Avoiding Attacking

Unless your purpose is to provoke followup opinions to your presentation or to persuade your reader to a specific course of action as an absolute must, it works well to avoid attacking a person, place, or idea. Attacks can backfire. If the attack is too vicious, the reader can turn against the attacker and turn the page. Even when attack is used, if both sides of an issue are presented, usually the writing evokes a more desirable response. Writing with a sense of fairness is important.

• Personalities

When you avoid attacking, however, your work does not have to be limp, lifeless prose. You can take a stand. You can write with passion, but it will serve you well to write with precision. Research your topic from many angles, then focus on the aspect that excites you most and will appeal to your target audience. Nevertheless, present both sides of the story. Your work can sizzle with fantastic facts and figures. You can write with objectivity and accuracy. You can reveal motives, manners, and methods of noted personalities in big business, in the medical profession, in the legal profession, and in the sports world, to name a few.

You can paint portraits of the subjects and characters that populate your stories. You can show them from the outside in—their choices from the clothing they buy to the foods they favor to the friends they adore and the pets they keep. You can reveal their thoughts, their faiths, and their politics, and the whys that have set all these choices and qualities in motion.

You can support the general information that you offer with question-provoking quotations from the subject, stinging quotations from an opponent, and supporting words from family or friends. You can interweave expository quotations to delve deeper into the visions and emotions surrounding the situation of the subject and the subject's acquaintances.

An endless procession of figures—both known and emerging—about whom you can write are available. If you choose, you can expose scams, mortify perpetrators, and perhaps horrify onlookers and readers with what you discover from your careful research, and you can do your best to write all of it as objectively as you can.

Ron Franscell, winner of two illustrious awards—the Associated Press Managing Editors Freedom of Information Award and the National Newspaper Association FOI Prize—says, "News is seldom written as 'good' or 'bad.' It's true that reporters are humans, but almost all classically trained journalists are doggedly devout at setting aside their emotions and biases to write as fair and honest a report as humanly possible. . . . The only judgment of whether a story is 'positive' or 'negative' is made by the reader, who is typically not as adept at setting aside his biases as a trained reporter."

• Places

You can conduct your readers on a tour of the Egyptian pyramids. You can enlighten your readers about the vulnerability from floods that Dhaka, Bangladesh, endures due to its alluvial nature. You can enchant your readers with the ancient victories of past places or enlighten them about the needs of a struggling nation. You can compare geographic locations controlled by humankind, those untamed, and those where the treachery of nature's uncertainty looms.

• Ideas

You can discuss the pros and cons of cold fusion, the promising possibilities and considerable liabilities of cloning, and the tug-of-war between big businesses. Limitless topics are accessible for your meticulous researching and passionate writing. You can support your cause. You can reveal your mission.

Avoiding Overselling

When you write about "What Phytochemicals Can Do for You," if you can cite irrefutable research, you add credibility to your message. If you cite expert after expert who praises some topic yet neglects to mention some opposing research findings, then your reader may get the idea that you are overselling. If, on the other hand, you present both sides of an issue as objectively as possible and then succinctly summarize your findings or present the facts, and finish the article, but leave your reader ruminating on the outcome, you allow the reader to decide what is what.

Pleading with readers and grabbing them by their collars with the use of "we" constructions can work for some articles and some audiences when the writer directs the work to a tightly knit group with a common agenda. Many editors, though, specifically request that "we" not be used and quickly reject those typescripts that disregard that request. It is important to know what is used in your target publication so that you do not violate what the editor prefers.

For a vast general audience with multiple political, social, cultural, and spiritual backgrounds, it often serves the writer well to present the material and allow the reader to draw his own final conclusions.

Avoiding Overtelling

Presenting as many pertinent facts as necessary from both sides of an issue exhibits your integrity and builds your credibility. Presenting a logical flow of information that speeds your reader through an entertaining, yet informing, landscape of ideas to a succinct satisfying closure helps to endear readers.

The Ending

Amick of *First Word Bulletin* says that the ending is just as important as the beginning and the body. "A poor article seems to end when the writer runs out of ideas. A good ending ties up the loose ends positively. A recap of the main message just gives the story a weak ending. An ending can go back and answer a question brought up in the first paragraph, or leave the reader a strong point to ponder over." He suggests leaving a mind-expanding image, a heartfelt observation, a vivid contrast, or an unsettling question in the minds of the readers.

Amick says,

> I wrote a story once on bull fighting, and the last sentence read, 'Poetic justice? A tragedy or a national spectacle?' (The matador and the bull had died together.) That ending should have kept the reader wondering for a week. The only comment I received on that story was concerning that last sentence.

You can amuse and entertain or educate and enlighten readers on topics of interest to you. When you share with others what you have learned—with an honoring spirit—you can create bonds of friendship with your readers, even if that news is not the happy news they might crave. When you present balanced communications, though, and then allow your readers to make their own decisions, those bonds of friendship that are manifested may be quite enduring.

Think about the deeply felt words of novelist, Ron Franscell, editor of *News-Record*, who also has been published in the *Chicago Sun-Times, Christian Science Monitor,* and *Rocky Mountain News*:

Readers increasingly demand their news to be happy talk until they need a champion to point out unfair play and injustice. They complain about "bias" in reporting, but agitate for a "positive slant." They want there to be no sacred cows until their own ox is gored. And our competitor's dilemma is common: If a newspaper restricts itself only to happy talk, can it effectively comfort the afflicted? Can it champion important values such as free speech or honest discourse or just human decency? Can it have any integrity? My answer, unequivocally, is, 'No.'

It is not a good newspaper's job to devote itself to Chamber of Commerce boosterism. But every good newspaper is dedicated to making its community a better place to live, sometimes by acknowledging what is best and sometimes by illuminating what is worst.

If we cannot confront our shortcomings as a community, we have no meaningful future.

Freelance reporters must bring this same ethic to their work or risk being treated as an amateur. Nobody says you can't have feelings, but you must set them aside when writing news and feature material for your local newspaper. Good editors will demand fairness.

It's difficult—no, impossible—for a human being to be truly objective. We are sentient creatures who form ideas and opinions without consciously knowing we are. We choose this verb over that one, and by doing so, have allowed our biases to surface. The best we can do is to try to be as fair as possible by recognizing our biases, then set them aside to tell a balanced story.

So, as you try to launch your freelancing career, a better way to view your local newspaper is as a mirror. It should reflect a true image of who we are. It should not hide our blemishes nor distort our charms.

That's how we'll know the truth. And that's the only way we can honestly build on our strengths and repair our weaknesses.

● ● ●

If a writer truly wants to contribute to *Continental* magazine, persistence pays off. The first—and most important—step is to discuss the editorial calendar with me. Not only does it show enthusiasm on your part, it helps me get a feel for your strengths. . . .

Ken Beaulieu
CONTINENTAL
Boston, MA

The most effective thing a writer can do to grab my attention is to tell me what sets her topic apart from others and why that topic will be of value to our readers.

Karen Menehan
MASSAGE MAGAZINE
Santa Cruz, CA

My biggest beef is with writers who insist that their story is right for our magazine when they obviously have never read it.

Sara Gilbert
U.S. ART
Minneapolis, MN

The staff enjoys working with freelancers; but all too frequently we receive queries and transom pieces that simply have no relevance to our publication.

Carol Schaal
NOTRE DAME MAGAZINE
Notre Dame, IN

Chapter 15.
Writing with a Purpose Pays

A systematic plan cannot insure a successful holiday party, but it certainly can move your party a giant step in the right direction. A smooth holiday party can reunite old friends, introduce new friends, and create a pleasant memory for you and all your guests.

Tradewind
Winter 1995

The introduction of my article "Planning a Great Holiday Party" offers an honest assessment of what planning ahead and preparing throughtfully for a party can bring. In Chapter 7, "Maximizing Your Research," you can recall that I mentioned several useful ways to develop your articles. To reiterate a few approaches, I noted chronological or hierarchical development. I included organizing by priority and by describing and developing your materials by moving the reader from general to specific information or from specific data to general notions. I also suggested inviting your reader through how-to steps to enlighten or to entertain or showing your reader by cause and effect.

"Planning a Great Holiday Party" for *Tradewind* in Curaçao, Netherlands Antilles, practically wrote itself through a blueprint that included somewhat of a combination of date, priority, general to specific, and how-to steps.

Planning a Great Holiday Party

Planning Ahead

　　Three to four weeks in advance

Pre-Party Task List for a Do-It-Yourself Party

　　Two weeks in advance
　　One week in advance
　　Three or four days in advance
　　One day in advance
　　The day of the party

The Party

The tone throughout the article was light-hearted and festive. A more somber tone works well for articles bursting with more serious information.

It has been estimated that approximately 45,000 people are victims of acute poisoning from pesticides in the United States annually, and as many as 3,000 people are affected profoundly enough to require hospitalization.

Maryland Maturity Lifestyles
June 1996

These opening words of my modest, but informative, article, "Enjoy a Pest-free Haven," introduce a significant problem to readers. Obviously, the article is prepared for a distinct group—those interested in home and garden and health. Intrigued readers probably will read beyond the hook. They will read to see what the article promises. They even may read the article in its entirety.

Grabbing the Attention of Your Readers

If you fascinate your readers with a topic that intrigues them, you should be able to hold their interest if you make your destination clear, organize well, and write with a purpose.

Effective options to pesticides are known and available. Some are old and time-tested. Others are new and appear in the current pages of science and technology journals.

Showing Your Route

The preceding sentence, also from the same article, discloses the organization and direction of the article.

Enjoy a Pest-free Haven

Before Pesticides

Eliminate Entryways

Eliminate Enticements

Serving Suggestions

Preventing Pet Food Problems

Pesticide Problems

Safer Pesticides

Ridding Your Home of Roaches

Shooing Away Ants

Galling Grain Pests

Fighting Flies

Foiling Fleas

A Safer Environment

These headings and subheadings served as "route markers" for the article. While some editors dislike alliteration, others use it to add a catchiness that helps the readers to remember the content. Find out what your editor likes by studying past issues of her magazine. Do not just make your work sing, make it harmonize with what she prefers.

If you make your destination clear so that your readers know where you intend to take them, your writing will be more appealing. If you organize logically and point the way with route markers—section headings and even subheadings, if needed—you blaze a trail. When you point out interesting sights along the way, engage the readers' senses of hearing and smelling and touching, you enhance their trip. Your logical organization and purposeful writing save time for busy readers today.

To match the publication which uses statistics and quotes from authorities, for this report, I also shared statistics and recommendations from experts.

Matching Your Market

Reports

For some publications, you may just write a report giving the facts gathered from researched information and quotes from outstanding experts. Your report could be on a topic such as the history of DDT, the first chlorinated organic insecticide, originally prepared in 1873.

Profiles

Or perhaps you could turn your report into a profile. With a bit of a new focus, you could write about Paul Muller, who discovered the effectiveness of DDT as an insecticide in 1939 and was honored for his discovery with the Nobel Prize in 1948.

If he left an autobiography, you could quote from that. You also could offer quotes from his letters and journals. You could include his own words that showed his thoughts and beliefs and concerns. You could reveal what others thought of him and of his work. You could quote from biographies.

If you prepare a profile on a living scientist, then you could add quotes directly from the scientist to convey his or her thoughts and feelings.

History Pieces

Either of your stories—the history of DDT and the profile of Paul Muller—may be able to qualify as a history piece, because both report on an historical event and both require substantial research to collect interesting, yet bona fide, information.

Investigative Articles

You might even turn your DDT piece into an investigative article by delving into the opposing positions regarding this substance. You could elaborate that on one side, DDT was heralded for saving millions of lives in the 1950s and promised to wipe out malaria forever. However, with curtailed use around the world and a ban on its use in the United States in 1973, a resurgence of malaria is taking the lives of millions of people annually in third world countries, especially.

Yet, others are calling for a worldwide ban on DDT. Their side of this difficult picture arises from the fact that the chemical stability of DDT and its fat solubility poses a health hazard. DDT is stored in the fatty tissues of humans and animals, and it takes about eight years for a human or an animal to metabolize it.

When you prepare an article on a controversial topic, it is important to present both sides of the issue. Authorities from both camps often are eager to speak. It will be your difficult task to wade through their agendas and present a piece as objectively as you can.

Service Articles

You might enjoy composing a piece on "Checking Your Prescriptions" or "Pros and Cons of a Glass Cooktop" or "Finding Fun Things to Do in Your Town." Service articles can range from extremely serious to gentler topics, and all call for a careful, up-to-the-minute collection of information.

Travel Stories

You might cover some day trips to exciting spots to explore just minutes away from your own backyard. Or you may get lucky and win an assignment to cover a grand resort in Spain, or you might fly to Egypt to do an article on "A Modern Day View of the Creation of the Pyramids." Or perhaps, you might cover a cruise to the beautiful Greek Isles.

Lynn Grisard Fullman, whom you first met in Chapter 9, "Improving Your Style," says, "As with all writing, it is important to use all your senses so you can describe all sorts of details of your travels, from the smell of baking bread to the sound of clanging trains or tinkling bells, the screech of tires, or a blinding light." She suggests finding time to jot notes to seize vivid images and impressions as you travel, for "Preserved, they make fine fodder for tales of travel."

Opinion Stories

If you are inclined to speak your mind, then you might enjoy doing an opinion piece. If you are steeped in your topic, then you simply may present your opinion and back it up with own data. If not, you can research the piece, compose it, and breathe into it the life that only you can give it. You might share your opinion on what drives the stock market on its rollercoaster ride, if you are a long-time broker. If not, still you can study the stock market from the inside out, delve into history and business and finance, study the approaches of the men and women at the helms of companies, and read about what creates volatility. You also can interview some well-known brokers, then organize and distill your information to define your opinion, which you will report.

Personal Experience Accounts

Perhaps you have a personal experience that will entertain and educate a general audience. Your story could be about anything. You could write about having won a new Chevy truck for that hole-in-one you shot at the American Red Cross fundraiser last month and how winning has created a new responsibility. Or you could tell about how you saved a tiny dachshund from being run over when a cruel person kicked him into the street, yet you were bitten because of your efforts. These creative nonfiction stories could be handled somberly or perhaps with just the right touch, even lightheartedly, depending on your audience and your purpose.

Humorous Stories

It is not difficult to see that you can turn a personal experience story into a humorous story. Also, depending on your handling of the material and matching your publication ever so carefully, you may even have an inspirational story that is infused with humor. More often, though, inspirational stories may bring a tear.

Inspirational Stories

Perhaps you have a knack for telling inspirational stories. You might compose an article about a group of citizens helping build a new home for a WWII veteran whose home was condemned and was about to be destroyed. Perhaps you could write an inspirational piece about a young Ph.D. candidate in Bangladesh tormented by the illiteracy rate of his country. You could carry the reader through his busy day of cleaning up the land after a recent cyclone, studying for his exams, and yet finding time to help teach youngsters and adults to read.

How-to Articles

If your editor appreciates how-to articles about cooking, perhaps you could submit your step-by-step instructions on how to make the perfect omelette the Julia Child way. You would be sure to talk about the freshness of the eggs, the ingredients added, the just right sprinkle of salt and pepper, the vegetable oil used, the cooking temperature, and the exact time to 'shake and jerk' the egg mixture. This story, too, can be either serious or humorous, depending on your audience and what you wish to convey.

Or you might guide readers through your most recent building project of nestled tables. You could outline cutting the legs, planing, tapering the legs, cross cutting, beveling, working on the sides, sanding, attaching the legs and side pieces, assembling the sides, clamping, and finally attaching the top. For some stories, if the editor appreciates them, you also will include supportive anecdotes. Certainly, for the building project, excellent photographs or transparencies will be a must, so take lots of photos to demonstrate your project step by step. Then choose your finest shots for submission.

First, find an editor who would appreciate such stories. Then query. When you receive your go-ahead, present the information logically and smoothly to engage your audience. You can be guided by sample articles in your target publications so that you have a feel for the depth and breadth of the materials presented and whether it dwells on somber topics or lighthearted ones or a blend of the two, or some other totally different tone.

If you study back issues of your target magazine, then you will be able to understand even more than the flow. You will be able to mesh the tone and essence of your work with the other articles of the publication. At the same time, you do not have to lose your own voice.

Regarding Voice

Vanessa Raphaely, the Editor of *Cosmopolitan* in Cape Town, whom you first met in Chapter 4, "Knowing Your Audience," says, "No magazine should have one voice. Good writing is a conversation, and magazines should not iron out the individuality of each writer's voice."

On the contrary, the Editor of *CATsumer Report* and *Good Dog!,* Judi Becker, whom you met in Chapter 2, "Getting on the Right Track," says, "The writer should read the publication in question and become familiar with its voice."

Once again, note the importance of knowing precisely what each editor prefers. Knowing subtle differences can mean the difference in landing assignment after assignment or receiving form rejection notes. The way to know these subtle differences is to study many issues of your target publications.

- Does your target magazine publish only business articles?
- Does it present a profile of a regional or national politician in each issue?
- Does it publish articles only on sports?
- Does your target publication run recipes?
- Does each issue include an automotive column?
- What is unique about your target magazine?
- What is the mission of your target magazine?
- What age range reads your target magazine?
- Just what makes your target magazine tick?

Study issue after issue until you understand the mission of the magazine. If you study the masthead and compare its staff listing with the bylines and find that your target publication is wide open to professional writers, you can solidify your purpose. You can find the just right topic to propose. You can determine its special slant, and you are well on your way.

Balancing Your Information

The headings and subheadings of "Enjoy a Pest-free Haven" shown above were developed reasonably. The article fit in nicely with surrounding articles.

Even though headings are great markers, if your target publication does not use them, then do not submit an article filled with these 'road signs.' Follow the pattern of your target magazine if you want your work published.

Your thoughts will move. Your ideas will link one to another like box-cars and end with your conclusion just as the train ends with its caboose.

Balancing your information is a bit like filling the boxcars uniformly.

If one section of your article outweighs your other components, you can trim it or embellish the other sections with additional relevant information for better balance. If the material under one heading is underdeveloped, you can add more data. If need be, you also can include subheadings to create greater balance.

Preparing a Sidebar

If you have supplementary information, but it really does not fit into the article, it may form the perfect sidebar. Many editors appreciate sidebars and often pay for them. If your editor does like sidebars, then prepare your sidebar carefully and submit it along with your article. You may be pleasantly surprised at the outcome.

For an editor who perhaps would be interested in the history of DDT and its being banned in the United States in 1973, I could have included a sidebar of five or 10 other chemicals whose use offers both positives and negatives for society.

Place sidebars following the text of your typescript and indicate that the information is offered for a sidebar or sidebars. To accompany a real estate article "Buying Your First Home," you might write a sidebar to accompany it such as "10 Tips for Deciding on a Real Estate Agent."

Sample Sidebar

10 Tips for Deciding on a Real Estate Agent
By (Your Name)

1. . . .
2. . . .
3. . . .
4. . . .
5. . . . etc.

This simple method of preparing a sidebar has worked for me as a writer, and I prefer it as an editor. Editors choose where the sidebar(s) will be placed, so placing sidebars at the end of your typescript is both polite and useful. If your writer's guidelines from your editor request a different approach, then follow the instructions of your particular editor.

On June 3, 1999, *BodyIsland* ran my sidebar "Shoe-Shopping Tips from the American Orthopaedic Foot and Ankle Society (AOFAS)" which also included "Sock-Shopping Tips from Thor•Lo—A Leader in Sport-Specific

Socks" as a feature article instead of as an accompaniment to my article "Style without Sacrificing Your Feet." So always prepare your sidebars just as carefully as you compose your articles. While many editors pay extra for sidebars, certainly if your editor publishes your sidebar as a feature, you should expect to be paid for it.

A Safer Environment

These methods of pest control should serve you well, for they not only will help to give you a pest-free haven, but also they will give you a safer environment. Far fewer toxins will be present in your home, because of your careful pesticide choices. With the health of thousands at stake, this modest approach to pest control is an invaluable measure.

Maryland Maturity Lifestyles
June 1996

"Enjoy a Pest-free Haven" goes back to basics, conveys details in plain English, and ends with a brief summary conclusion that this editor appreciates.

Accomplishing Your Mission

Harold Ort, Editor of *Popular Communications*, maintains, "It's not about glitzy photos or illustrations or trying to impress an editor with facts. Attract your editor's attention by going back to basics and include photos *with* captions."

When you show editors that you can rivet the attention of your readers, show your intended route, match your market, balance your information, and draw a conclusion, you will sell more articles. Remember, though, one major key to success is to find an editor who shares your vision and who appreciates the way you convey your common message. Writing with a purpose pays.

So look and listen, and absorb interesting bits of information from everywhere. Keep the ones that stick in your mind and won't seem to go away....

Nancy McAlary
WRITINGNOW.COM

We are always looking for a new twist on subject matter.

Lisa Rosenthal
SAN FRANCISCO PENINSULA
PARENT
San Francisco, CA

Chapter 16.
Finding a New Twist

If you are asking "Where should I look for ideas that publishers will buy?", most writers probably would suggest that you should read widely, observe, and listen. You will find an unending number of ideas to write about from "Preventing Teen Suicides" to "The Pros and Cons of Cloning" to "Why the World Loves Chocolate."

Lisa Rosenthal, Editor of *San Francisco Peninsula Parent*, whom you first met in Chapter 4, "Knowing Your Audience," says, "We are always looking for a new twist on subject matter. For example, every year we do an article on birthday parties. So new and creative birthday party ideas would get my attention. Trend articles and articles that touch on a timely issue are also attention grabbers."

Being Original

Raphaely, the Editor of *Cosmopolitan*, who shared her thoughts about voice in Chapter 15, "Writing with a Purpose Pays," says, "Set yourself high standards for originality, freshness, and relevance."

If your target publication has already done the piece you want to write, then tell the editor how your story is different. That is what Greg Jones of *Sailing* Magazine advises.

Managing Editor of *Notre Dame Magazine,* Carol Schaal, whom you met in Chapter 3, "Finding Your Dream Publications," says that ". . . . the biggest help of all is to pitch a refined story *idea*." Writers can achieve this task and increase their chances of acceptance by studying their publication to match their story ideas.

Shara Rendell-Smock, author of *Getting Hooked* and *Living with Big Cats*, says, "Any adventure can inspire an idea." She was inspired to write about animal training after seeing two 350-pound tigers seek affection from their trainer, David Tetzlaff, after their performance in Caribbean Gardens in Naples, Florida.

She says, "A gem of a project was screaming to me when I heard the cat show narrator announce that the Tetzlaff family had been in the animal business breeding endangered species, appearing on TV, and running a park and zoo for 35 years."

Finding New Topics and New Twists

Wendy McCallum says that writers who have done their homework first and have familiarized themselves with the position *Healthy Options* takes on health issues, a topic such as genetic engineering will stand out. She wants writers to realize, though, that studying just one issue of a target magazine is not enough.

Greg Jones of *Sailing* Magazine agrees and points out the importance of reading a year's worth of back issues to do your homework. He explains that it is crucial "to understand the annual flow of the publication."

Reading and studying from *Sailing* articles such as "A Reef, a Breeze, and Belize," by the editor himself, or "Navel of the World" by Martin Koning with photos by Susan Koning can begin your adventure to study the magazine in depth. Study every article. Immerse yourself in articles such as "Cruising the Forgotten Islands of the South Pacific," "Small-boat Adventures in a Big Sea," and "Small Lakes of the American West" from other issues, too. Keep reading. Still there are sections on Boat Tests, Boat Design, and Gear. Also read the News section and study their scads of ads to find a new twist.

Intriguing topics are all around you. Listen to people. Ask yourself what would interest your readers. Look for topics with universal appeal. A mere handful of questions follow to help you get started.

Thinking about Conversations People Share with You

- What is of compelling interest to your friends around the world?
- What did the airline passenger next to you have to say?
- What interests your tennis partner?
- What catches your hairstylist's attention?
- What did your supermarket clerk mention to you?
- When is your friend's next bridge tournament?
- What triggered a conversation with your child's orthodontist?

Thinking of Travel Ideas

- What city, state, or country did you just visit?
- Where will you be traveling next?

Lynn Grisard Fullman, who emphasized the importance of quickly recording your travel observations in Chapter 15, "Writing with a Purpose Pays," suggests, "Even if you're planning a general travel piece, look for what's new or what's coming—but avoid what's temporary, such as an exhibit that will be gone soon and would quickly date your material."

She recommends that writers take a close look at their own city as well as all the places they visit. She says, "Sometimes you have to look beyond the obvious. There's a story in everyone, and sometimes those stories can be woven neatly into travel stories that have twists that draw readers into your tales."

She also says to be alert for a human touch to spin into your story. "Listen to those around you. Did a taxi driver reveal something about the city? What did a store clerk mention to you? What did you overhear at the zoo?" She often uses such comments as captivating leads, for they can offer insight that brochures and press releases miss.

Thinking about Your Own City

Unique Qualities

- What is unique about your city? What is its main calling card?
- Why would visitors want to visit your city?
- Why is your city or state a leader in recycling, sock making, peach growing, guitar making, or some other topic that an editor would find appealing for his particular audience?
- Why is your city known especially for its volunteer spirit?
- Why has the crime rate of your city diminished during the last year?
- What can you say about your city's unique qualities?
- Why is your town supercharged or sleepy regarding politics?
- What forces lead your city?
- What special goals does your city have?
- Why is your city constantly astir with conventions?
- What special ways does your city have to prevent or handle pollution?
- Why is your city teeming with new industry?
- Which businesses are most prominent?
- What new ordinances are being put in place?
- How does your city nurture families and children?
- Why is your city a vacation spot for visitors?
- What brings the most revenue to your city?

Professions and Hobbies

- How many professions are represented in your town?
- How many different kinds of health care professions—traditional and complementary—are represented in your city?
- How is your city positively impacted by its university or universities?
- How is your town negatively impacted if it has no universities?
- How many art galleries and museums are in your city?
- Which museum is your city's oldest and finest?
- How long has a unique bootmaker, swordmaker, or candy kitchen been in your city?
- How many computer businesses are in your city?
- Who among your friends have interesting collections?
- What hobbies or recreational activities are represented by clubs and organizations in your city—gardening, quilting, knitting, boat making, touring, kayaking, spelunking, mountain climbing, repelling, or bungee jumping?

Thinking about Personalities in Your City

- Who is the youngest or oldest doctor, lawyer, pharmacist, naturopath, or acupuncturist in your city?
- Who are your favorite athletes? Interview them.
- What are your neighbor's unique talents?

Entertainment

- Which sports are your favorites?
- How many fitness centers thrive in your city?
- How many golf courses does your city boast?
- How does your racetrack impact your city's economy?
- Why is your city a leader in pet shows?
- When is the next rodeo coming to your town?
- Where can you go in your town to take horseback riding lessons?
- What games enchant your children?

- Which holidays reverberate with activity in your city?
- Would your city's calendar of events enthrall readers? Where? Why? Which publication would be interested in which event?
- Which magazines are published in your city?

Food
- Who among your friends is a wine connoisseur?
- Who among your friends is a gourmet cook?
- What favorite recipes can you or your club share?

Purchases
- Do you have special budgeting tips you can offer?
- Can you write about your time-saving shopping tips?

You can use any one of these questions as a springboard then create a new twist for a future article.

Finding a New Twist for Short Stories, Too

Secrets from a Successful Romance Writer

Co-author Nancy McAlary, of Brisbane, Australia, launched her career as a fiction writer in 1996, and since then she has sold several dozen short stories to magazines in Australia, New Zealand, South Africa, the United Kingdom, and the United States.

Regarding getting new twists for her stories, she says, "Because my genre is grounded in real, everyday situations, that is exactly where I look for my inspiration. I read the newspaper, listen to snatches of conversation in supermarkets, and watch television a bit. Sometimes one tiny snippet of information can be turned into a twist on the traditional boy-meets-girl plot."

Nancy goes on to say, "A recent story that I sold to two different editors on two different continents had a heroine who was hired to go to a company's social evening, pretend to be a new employee, get a little tipsy and flirt with the boss as a bit of a joke. Unfortunately, she selects the wrong "target," is attracted to him, and one thing leads to another until her identity is revealed and everything ends happily.

"Sounds implausible, doesn't it? But I got the germ of the idea from an interview I read with an aspiring actress who does exactly that here in Australia to make some part-time money—hires herself out to company parties, masquerades as a new employee, and pretends to get inebriated to loosen everybody up. Truth, as they say, is stranger than fiction.

"So look and listen, and absorb interesting bits of information from everywhere. Keep the ones that stick in your mind and won't seem to go away. Ask 'What if?'

"And I'll give you one other little tip to get you started—buy a few women's magazines with advice or help columns where readers write in to tell about their problems. These letters are about real relationships, and real emotions, and there is a fortune in seminal ideas in these letters just waiting to be unearthed." Perhaps Nancy's method will work for you, too, if you write fiction.

Being Given Ideas

Occasionally fans send Fern Michaels suggestions for topics they would like to see her develop into a novel. She said that such was the case for *Dear Emily* and *Wish List*.

Sometimes readers suggest ideas for nonfiction works, as well. After reading my *BodyIsland* articles on periodontal health, Pat Warren of Zimbabwe wrote to me to suggest another dental article.

Creating Balance

After you determine new twists and begin developing them, if you write nonfiction, perhaps it may help to consider what I said in Chapter 13, "Balancing Your Communication:"

One-sided arguments can irritate readers and cause them to flip the page to find a more objective article. In most cases, of course, the article never will reach print because a great many editors will reject such articles. Out-of-balance articles usually are guilty on any number of counts—attacking, overselling, and overtelling.

So, whatever your new twist, remember to develop the idea fully and with clarity. Editors are interested in breakthroughs in science, health, automobiles, fashion, baby care, and geriatric care, to mention only a few. They are interested in "tomorrow's" news. The editor will not touch a "rehash" query or typescript for more than the time that it takes to read the title and the first few words. That editor may stop before the punctuation mark at the end of the first sentence. So if you have something to say, it must be earthshaking. If it is on a much-addressed topic, your slant must be unique. You cannot expect to send your work two weeks after an event, have it lie in a slush pile for two months, then see it published three months later. It is old news.

Unless your unique slant produces new insight, promotes a panoramic vision that surpasses the thousands of articles that already have been published and the many other thousands in ever-mounting slush piles, your work will not be published. Your passion, no matter how deep and genuine it is, will have a tough time being marketed if you must compete with every top journalist in the world, who has access to every piece of up-to-the-minute groundbreaking news. Think about the importance of thoughtful timing. Tailor your queries and submissions with care and time them to meet your particular editor's needs.

Planning Ahead for the Next Time

If you miss the mark because of poor timing, yet you think you have a great story to share, you always can hold your story and continue to work on it and polish it. Then submit your updated query or the updated typescript—if appropriate to your target publication—three to six months before the anniversary of the birth or the death of the celebrity or the anniversary of the event to give your piece a chance in the next round of competition. Again, it is an absolute must to know the lead time of your target magazine to pave your path to an acceptance for your article. Timing is an element that must not be overlooked if you wish to boost your writing sales.

Meeting Deadlines

Another important element of timing is that of meeting deadlines. Greg Jones of *Sailing* Magazine, who has offered numerous suggestions to steer the readers of *The Writer's Friend* away from problems with editors, says, "The only thing more important in the world of freelancing than writing talent is making deadlines. It is a depressing reflection of people's discipline that editors often are forced to use writers who are good enough but who always make their deadlines when they have brilliant writers who cannot be bothered to get things in on time. The magazine will go out. It must go out, and if it means using someone not as good as but whose work is there, then so be it."

I find that it is an excellent plan always to meet deadlines a bit early, if possible. Punctuality certainly pleases editors. I wrote a monthly column for Howard Jardine, Editor of *Balance Fitness* in London, England, from May 1996 until December 1998, and usually submitted articles in groups of four or six at a time to be helpful to him with his scheduling. He once told me, "This really does help with planning ahead. I am nearly always waiting for articles to arrive up to the last minute, so this is extremely helpful."

So keep querying and writing and submitting on time. Also, keep in mind your abundant opportunities with multiple noncompeting publications when you sell one-time print rights or simultaneous print rights or first print rights but are careful to retain reprint rights. Good luck with finding new twists and with cultivating impeccable timing!

• • •

Chapter 17.
Cooperating with Editors

Anthony Mark Dalessandro, former Editor of *Italian America*, who shared information in Chapters 3 and 8, says that writers "need to be more patient, considerate, and polite. It's amazing how rude some writers are to prospective editors."

Courteous writers who do team up with editors reach this exciting goal by becoming knowledgeable about their target publications so that they can market with precision. They also pay attention and follow editors' instructions and requirements. Astute writers also maintain excellent writing standards, never argue with editors, and keep their promises. Rather than arguing with an editor. Find another editor. Find an editor whose mission you support.

Being Informed

Wendy McCallum, Co-Editor of *Healthy Options*, whom you last met in Chapter 16, says, "We are much more likely to give ongoing work to someone with specialist experience or knowledge. If the writer does not have this training, they need to show they can liaise with the industry experts, best done by way of submission of a researched (therefore accurate) and sufficiently in-depth article that introduces new information to the reader and makes for an interesting read."

Research and interviews can supply ample information for some topics for some editors, but there are other editors who need writers who know their subject inside and outside and up and down from practical experience. The information must flow from their writers as freely as sweat from a cowboy in the broiling desert sun.

Mark Kalan, Editor of *CC Motorcycle NewsMagazine*, Nyack, New York, says, "If you don't know anything about motorcycles—don't write for me." He sticks by the familiar advice, "Write about what you know."

Targeting Carefully

Don't waste time submitting materials to editors who will not appreciate your work. Submit a query only after poring over many sample copies of your target publication and recognizing that what you propose will suit the magazine.

Gena Holle, Editor of *The International Railway Traveler*, whom you met in Chapter 3, "Finding Your Dream Publications," says that *IRT* does not pay a lot, but it attracts a high caliber of writers who love trains and everything about them. She says, "Our writers and the trains are our lifeblood, because without them, *IRT* wouldn't exist." She also has "an eclectic core of editors from around the globe who are experts in various areas of rail, who offer a unique perspective about rail and rail politics that other publications lack. They do it because they feel so strongly about rail, not only as a great way to travel, but because it's such a fascinating part of the world's social fabric." So if you love trains, and you can write well, think of the exciting possibilities in store for you.

Find editors who share your passions and who champion your causes. Then make yourself not only available but also indispensable. The possibilities are teeming. Lisa Rosenthal, Editor of *San Francisco Peninsula Parent*, says, "Professional writers are our lifeblood!" She believes that the quality of the writing is the key to a successful magazine. She says, "We try to treat our writers fairly by paying them on time and working with them every step of the way."

Explore the newsstands and market guides and ask your writer friends about cordial editors. Also, wherever you go, notice the particular magazines people are reading on subways, trains, airplanes, or cruise ships. Possibly these are some of the markets waiting for you.

Studying Writer's Guidelines

Many publications do not permit unsolicited submissions by postal service or by e-mail. You must not violate their wishes. If your target publication supplies writer's guidelines by postal service or by e-mail, be sure to request a copy. If your target publication has writer's guidelines online, read those requirements to know how to submit your work, and follow the instructions.

The following question cannot be overemphasized.

What special requirement is given in the writer's guidelines of your target magazine that is not given in your various market guides?

Always find the answer to this question. If additional requirements are shared in the writer's guidelines, it pays to know.

Submitting Work Only as Requested

In Chapter 5, "Preparing to Query," I suggested that you send only what the publisher requests and send your work by whatever means the publisher requires—a hard copy 'query only' first, a hard copy query with sample clips, a hard copy of the complete typescript, a copy on disk in the platform the editor prefers, 'query only' first by e-mail, or complete typescript or story by e-mail. This tip is of utmost importance, if you wish to get along well with editors.

Often students ask, "Well, couldn't I just send...?"

The answer is "Send exactly what the editor requires based on what you know from the writer's guidelines supplied by your editor." You will wave a red flag if you frivolously "just send" whatever you please. Your packet will be received just like the "charred chunk of meat" described in Chapter 13, "Grabbing An Editor's Attention."

Be cooperative. Send e-mail submissions only to publications that permit e-mail submissions, and send them according to the editor's preference— in the body of the message or as an attachment. You will find such submission requirements in writer's guidelines. Just because a publication has an e-mail address does not mean that the editor accepts e-mail submissions. Amick of *First Word Bulletin* in Madrid is among many editors who lament that "Writers send 25-page submissions by e-mail without permission."

If you send an article by e-mail to a publisher who does not wish to receive submissions by e-mail, you can imagine deletion with one click.

When you do submit by e-mail to editors who welcome such submissions, always format your work carefully to accommodate your editor. Send your best work with painstaking syntax, meticulous spelling, correct grammar, and appropriate tone for your audience.

Paying Attention to Word Count

Holle of *IRT* says, "Not sticking to the word counts is the most glaring faux pas writers make. When we say no more than 1,400 words for a feature, including sidebar, that's what we mean! It's amazing how many writers send us 3,000-, or even 4,000-word, stories, then expect us to edit them to fit our format."

If you think that Holle is alone. Think again. Jim Adair, the Editor-in-Chief of *Homes & Cottages*, who shared tips in Chapters 2 and 4, also says, "Don't pitch a 3,000-word essay to a magazine that runs nothing more than 700-word articles. You'd be amazed how often this happens."

Keeping Submission Standards High

Even if you think it is boring to follow the writing rules and regulations of editors, if you wish to be a published writer, it is prudent to obey the time-tested standards.

Your laser-printed typescript on 25% cotton bond paper in a basic mono-spaced font should be free of errors, and it should be crisp and clean. If your typescript is sprinkled with handwritten corrections, arrows indicating section changes, and explanatory notes attached, and it looks like your new puppy or kitten slept on it, your typescript goes up to bat with three strikes against it. Editors appreciate materials free of errors and in good shape.

Cosmopolitan Editor, Vanessa Raphaely, of Cape Town, reminds writers, "Cut out every unnecessary adjective, and kill every cliché. Research, substantiate, research, research. Check spelling and phone numbers. Send in clean copy."

Travel from Raphaely's office in Cape Town to Lisa Rosenthal's editorial office in San Francisco, and you will find the same sentiment. It is most important to Rosenthal, as an editor, that an article be well-written and well-researched and that the writer is familiar with the style and content of her magazine.

Editors appreciate writers who use excellent grammar and syntax, punctuate properly, and spell meticulously. Editors in academic journal offices grimace to see typescripts with sloppy spelling, subject—verb agreement errors, misnumbered footnotes, incorrectly formatted bibliographies, and misnumbered citations. Such flagrant errors not only are discourteous to the editors, but also they are a disservice to the neophytes uninformed enough to submit such typescripts. Editors are even more infuriated when writers who are known to have writer's guidelines in their hands try to slip through rushed, haphazard writing.

Some academic journal offices put up with such nonsense and have editors waste hours reworking articles. More than likely, though, paying publications will flip such submissions into a mounting stack of rejections. It is true. Note what McCallum of New Zealand says, "Submissions of articles that are going to need considerable in-house work to get up to standard—concising and beefing up with further research—are unlikely to be accepted."

Julia Bencomo Lobaco, the Editor of *Vista* in Coral Gables, Florida, says, "An otherwise salable article on a fascinating topic could be doomed by errors, which make the potential buyer wary of the entire product's integrity, not just the poorly written portions."

Debbie Ridpath Ohi, Editor of *Inklings*, says, "Other instant 'turn-offs' include spelling and grammar errors in their queries, starting their queries with 'Dear Sir,' and using attachments instead of sending their queries in the body of the e-mail messages."

Be responsible. Never submit half-done work and expect an editor to do your work for you. Write, then proofread, prune, and polish. Then put your typescript away for a few days. Take it out and read it aloud. Reorganize, rewrite, and rework it, if need be. Make your typescript sing by varying sentence lengths and creating smooth transitions. Build toward a logical conclusion. When submitting to editors who allow e-mail submissions, follow their writer's guidelines with care.

You may recall that Editor G.W. Amick, of *First Word Bulletin,* said in Chapter 13, "Grabbing an Editor's Attention," that he often could form an accurate opinion about a writer's work just from the appearance of their envelope." So be apprised that first impressions are important and enduring. Style, too, is important, of course. Amick explains that while the first paragraph is very important, the body of your story sells it. He says, "The sentences must be short. They must make me want to read more, like a mystery story does. The writer's thought patterns will help him or her move on smoothly and logically from one aspect to the next and ensure that nothing is left out."

Similarly, Joseph Sherman, the former Editor of *Jewish Affairs,* says, "Above all, the style of the piece should be clear, direct, free of clichés, hackneyed expressions, and pretentious posturing."

M.J. Van Deventer, the Editor of *Persimmon Hill* says, "Submissions should have been proofed not only by the writer, but also by the person who is the subject of the article before it lands on my desk."

If you are privy to behind-the-scenes thoughts and words of editors from around the world, you will hear the same laments. The words of Lobaco sum up their irritations, "One of my pet peeves is receiving sloppy work." She admonishes, "Check your spelling and grammar." She warns, "Poorly written work will make an editor question a writer's reporting skills and accuracy."

It just may be safe to surmise that if you could visit every editorial office around the world, you would find that the same sentiment prevails.

Never rush a rough draft to an editor then interrupt the editorial process with intermediate revisions. Editors do not appreciate such submissions.

Try always to give accurate information. Check and double check your material for typographical errors, transpositions, or any inadvertent errors before submitting it. Read it. Proof it. Read it again after corrections.

If you find an error in fact, or if an expert or interviewee sends you a modification in a quote after you have posted, faxed, or e-mailed your submission, contact the editor with the correction as promptly as you possibly can. While it may be somewhat upsetting to you or to your editor at the moment, getting the correct information printed is of utmost importance. Your effort and good intentions should be appreciated.

Revising

As a bit of an aside about revision, let me tell you about an experience that former Editor Joseph Sherman and Sonia Pressman Fuentes—one of the founders of the National Organization for Women (NOW), a lawyer, writer, and public speaker—shared. Fuentes' "Getting an Article Published" that described this experience first appeared on *WritingNow.com* (September 1998) Vol. 02, No. 09.

Being a perfectionist and striving for excellence, each time Fuentes read her article that she had submitted to Sherman, [she] "saw ways to improve it and sent changes to Joseph." At one point, he responded, "It is always fatal to allow contributors to make changes after acceptance." Another time, he wrote, "You will see no more of it till it's published, else you'll be writing and re-writing forever."

When she finally wrote that she thought the piece was . . . good, Sherman responded, "After about four rewrites and three copy edits, it should be. If you make these many changes in your memoirs, it will either cost you a fortune, lose you the [book] contract, or make you a lifelong enemy of the publisher."

She replied, "Who cares about any of that if it improves the memoirs?" In April 1998, "Three United States Feminists: A Personal Tribute," written by Sonia Pressman Fuentes and edited by Joseph Sherman, was published in *Jewish Affairs*.

Sherman pointed out that "the revisions he permitted Fuentes to make were exceptions, and that normally he expected authors to submit pieces for consideration in final form."

Even though everything worked out well for Fuentes and Sherman, beginning writers must recognize this precarious position. Editors, in general, are not in the mood for a tennis match of endless serves and returns. Be forewarned.

Cautioning Beginning Writers

To reiterate, beginning writers, especially, should proceed with caution. Most editors want to receive only a final, well-polished typescript and do not cope well with perfectionistic writers who perhaps would revise interminably, if permitted. So write, then let your material rest. Read it again. Revise, revise, revise. Let it rest again, if time permits. Then read and revise your work more as needed before submitting your final polished version.

Getting Along with Editors

Scott Edelman, Editor of *Sci-Fi Entertainment*, Reston, Virginia, says, "Writers should learn that there's nothing personal involved. I get queried by dozens more writers than I could ever possibly use, and if I don't choose them it isn't a slighting of their worth. They should take rejection in a professional manner, knowing that they're in it for the long haul, and even though I pass them up now I might have a need for them later. They should worry more about planting the seeds for a career than investing all their hopes and energies on a single story."

He explains, "They should not attempt to argue me into taking a story, or lecture me on why I am wrong to turn them down, or tell me what a lousy magazine I publish and how their writing could improve it, or any number of amateurish behaviors. (And believe me—I am not joking with these examples.) Once the answer is 'no' they should accept it graciously, so that the next time they query, I will listen with an open mind."

Once you have a go-ahead from an editor, remember that it is important to stay within the framework of development for the article that you and your editor have set. Denise Castañon, the former Managing Editor of *Estylo* Magazine, Los Angeles, California, says, "Expect rewrites. No matter how good you think your piece is your editor will probably find something to change, especially if you didn't work closely with your editor. Rewrites are not punishment. Your editor is just trying to get the best story for the publication. Communication is essential. After initially talking to your editor repeat what you think she said. Ask questions. I prefer that a writer call me back repeatedly than to get a story I did not expect."

Phoning, If Invited

Even though Castañon shared her time generously with her writers, some editors despise phone interruptions. Always find out an editor's phone policy before you telephone. It is a good rule of thumb never to phone an editor unless you have been invited to do so.

Some editors, though, will invite you to phone them after having worked with them. They may even suggest that you telephone to present some of your hot topics as they emerge. It is important to earn this privilege.

Keeping Your Promises

Complete your submissions as planned and as promised and within the confines of the editor's designated word limit and other special instructions. Stay on track. When you and your editor have discussed and agreed upon a path for your article, don't blaze some other trail and send her the article. She will not be pleased.

Early in your preparation, if you sincerely believe that a different angle would be more viable and you feel that you must approach her with the idea to change your direction, proceed with caution, even if you have worked for the editor many times before. She may have graphic designers and illustrators working already to prepare companion artwork to accompany what she has clearly defined as your part of the project.

Essay

If your target publisher is expecting an essay from you, share your experience in first person with zest to entertain or educate your reader.

Magazine Feature

If you have promised a feature story for a magazine editor, submit your focused, carefully crafted work with your grab-your-reader-by-the-collar hook, your proposition and supporting argument, and clear conclusion. Build your feature with spicy quotes from interviews with people who can substantiate your claims, from your own experience and observations, and from library and online research.

If onlookers or involved persons offer choice words on your topic, give them a voice in your piece, too. Not only experts and celebrities boost reader interest. Sign-carrying picketers often can add as much zest to your feature as the CEO, whose company they are picketing. Words from both sides of the argument also can add not only variety but also balance. Finish with a riveting conclusion.

Magazine Filler

If you submit a brief filler, pack it with a powerful punch. Use vigorous verbs. Give the piece zing. It may be small, but it can be radiant.

Newspaper Editorial

If you submit an editorial that you know will be welcomed by your target newspaper, make your stand with clarity and punch to pull your readers to your special cause.

Newspaper Feature

If you have promised to submit a news feature to a newspaper editor, remember to disclose the who, what, when, where, why, and how of your story succinctly and swiftly as soon as you come up to bat. Pack the important information into your first couple of paragraphs. Trickle in the remaining useful information. Include the information of lesser significance for the finish. Then if your editor must cut off your last paragraph or two to fit your story into the issue, your audience still reads a good, solid story.

Being a Successful Writer

Paying attention pays. Writers who consider their editors' wishes and cooperate to create their articles receive more assignments, sell more articles, and are paid more. Remember, too, Aesop's words, "He that always gives way to others will end in having no principles of his own."

Instead of battling with an editor, though, find an editor who believes in your cause. Avoid calamities. Thinking through your writing projects and querying from a well-informed position can keep you light years ahead of the negligent and haphazard pencil pusher who is haunted by repeated rejections. So keep thinking and acquiring useful information and querying and completing assignments and submitting promptly to sell, sell, sell.

• • •

I have found that 'a picture is worth a thousand words.' To grab my attention, show me what you can do, plain and simple. The picture can be something you made or a picture of a drawing that shows what you plan on making.

Robert Joseph
WEEKEND WOODCRAFTS
Concord, CA

Even if the financial return for an accepted article may not compensate the initial time and effort put in, I suggest making that extra effort to impress the editor and get your writer's foot in the door.

Wendy McCallum
HEALTHY OPTIONS
Tauranga, New Zealand

[Writers] should take rejection in a professional manner, knowing that they're in it for the long haul, and even though I pass them up now I might have a need for them later. They should worry more about planting the seeds for a career than investing all their hopes and energies on a single story.

Scott Edelman
SCI-FI ENTERTAINMENT
Reston, VA

Chapter 18.
Finding out about Editors, Employment Agencies, and Technical Writers

By Joseph Gregg

Technical writing is communication that is geared toward a particular audience, such as new users of an accounting software program. The purpose of technical writing is to help users solve a problem or perform a task.

You find technical writing in a variety of fields. Examples of technical writing include:

- Software user manuals
- Installation guides for electronics, such as VCRs
- FDA reports from biotech companies
- Automotive maintenance manuals
- Directions for playing board games
- Recipes

Technical writing is strictly factual. You're there to tell someone how to do something. As a result, it's rather formulaic. In technical writing courses, you learn how to present information in an easy-to-use format. If you want someone to do a task sequentially, you use a numbered format. You also learn how to use graphics to increase understanding, such as providing a picture of the computer screen after the user performs a step.

Technical writing is challenging. You have to learn everything about the system you will be documenting and then write well enough so that users can learn the system quickly and easily. You also get to be on the cutting edge of technology, particularly if you work in the software industry. Furthermore, you have to keep improving your skills if you want to stay employed.

I've been a technical writing contractor for over seven years. I contract through agencies, who place me with companies for anywhere from a few weeks to a few years. My background is in software technical writing. Most of the manuals I write are for a technical audience, such as software developers. I've written most of my manuals for personnel of the company I was working for or for suppliers of the company. I have never written a manual for a software package that gets sold in stores. For most of my writing assignments, I have been the sole technical writer.

Technical Writing and the Editing Process

Companies such as Microsoft and IBM have formalized documentation processes. They have teams of writers who work on different chapters of the same manual. They also have teams of editors who edit the writers' work. However, in my experience, most technical writers are not so lucky. They may work on a team where each writer composes a manual and informally edits each other's work, or they may serve as the only writer on staff.

Most technical writers have three avenues for getting their manuals edited: other writers, subject matter experts (such as software developers), and themselves. Each avenue has its pros and cons.

Using Other Writers

If you're lucky enough to work with other writers, you should have them edit your work (and you should edit theirs). Writers understand the importance of editing. They know that another pair of eyes can usually catch errors that they've missed. Depending on the type of manual you're writing, other writers can edit it for grammar, style, content, or all three.

For example, if you're writing an end-user manual, where the users are not subject matter experts, the writers can review content, style, and grammar. Most end user manuals have procedures and concepts. The concepts usually describe the idea behind the procedure. If the writers can't understand the concepts or procedures, you can bet the end users won't either.

If you're writing a manual for subject matter experts and the other writers are unfamiliar with the subject, you can have them edit the manual for grammar and style. They should probably skip the conceptual material. If you're writing a C programming manual but the writers don't understand C, they're not going to understand the underlying concepts of the language. You should leave the conceptual material to the software developers.

Other writers can make sure your document styles, such as headers and bulleted text, are consistent. When you write, you tend to get sloppy. You're too busy writing to worry about format. Other writers can step back and check whether your heading style on page three matches that on page 133.

Writers usually hold meetings to determine document style. In these meetings, they develop templates that all writers must use to make all the company's documents consistent. This leads to professional looking documents and makes the writing process easier for new writers coming on board.

Using Subject Matter Experts

Subject matter experts are best at editing conceptual material. Because they have a solid understanding of the subject, they'll know if what you're saying is true. I'll talk about software engineers in this section because I have dealt with them for all of my writing assignments.

If you're writing a highly technical document, you need to have subject matter experts edit it. For example, say you're writing a document that describes how a financial application is designed. The document is for new software developers who join your company. The developers who designed the application need to edit your document for content. Otherwise, the new developers may get incorrect information. They'll then have to relearn the application before they can edit the code. This causes the company to lose time and money, all because your document wasn't edited.

Some developers also may try to edit your document for grammar. Usually, it's best to omit their corrections, unless the omission will leave the underlying conceptual material incorrect. Developers are not writers, though I've had some who considered themselves closet grammarians. Developers tend to write everything in the passive voice; and as every good technical writer knows, the active voice is better. It leads to shorter sentences and better comprehension. Developers also like to string nouns together, leaving sentences incomprehensible. They're also notorious for writing run-on sentences.

When you're writing conceptual material, you may be tempted to run to the developers every time you are stuck. Developers are busy people. If you keep asking them questions, they'll think you're a pest. Therefore, before you go asking them questions about conceptual material, see if you can find the answers for yourself, such as by reading the code, reading any existing literature, or playing with the application a little bit more.

If you can't read code, learn to read it. This is especially important if you'll be writing design documents and programmer's guides. Buy a book or take a seminar or class. In the long run you'll benefit for two reasons. One, you'll work faster because you won't have to bug the developers all the time. Two, you'll be more valuable to the company and possibly make more money.

Read everything you can about the application. Usually, the developers write functional specifications for the application before they start coding. Sure, the developers wrote them, so they won't be literary masterpieces. But you will get a general understanding of the application. Also, as part of the development team, you usually have a test, or beta, version of the application on your computer. Play with the application some more before you go running to the developers. You may have missed something the first time around.

Editing Documents Yourself

If you're the sole writer in your group, you're stuck with writing and editing. Though the developers may help edit the conceptual parts of your document, you're left editing the style and grammar.

As the sole writer, you have freedom and responsibility. You can develop your own document templates and styles without having to wait for a committee to decide on the standards. However, you have to make sure all your documents follow the templates. You may have a tendency to add new styles to your documents on the fly, making the templates obsolete.

It's fairly easy to edit your own documents for grammar. You can use books to help you out, such as *The Elements of Style* and *The Microsoft Manual of Style for Technical Publications*. However, it's tougher to edit your document for flow, such as determining if your topics follow each other in a logical order. Flow tends to be subjective, so if you're the only one doing the editing, the users of the manual are stuck with your logic.

You also can edit step-by-step procedures fairly easily. Just try to do the procedures yourself. If you can't, you need to rewrite the procedure. However, because you wrote the document and are more familiar with the application than an end user would be, you may inadvertently leave a step out or assume that the user knows what prior conditions need to be met before they start the procedure. When writing procedures, you have to hold the user's hand and detail every step.

When you're editing your document, you may read more into a sentence or paragraph than is actually there. Again, this is because you're too familiar with the subject. You have to learn to be an objective reader by pretending you're a new user. It takes practice to do this and not all writers can. I have trouble myself sometimes, even though I've been writing technical manuals for seven years.

Another drawback to editing your own work is that it gets boring. After writing a manual, the last thing you want to do is read and edit it. It gets even more boring after the third or fourth time. This boredom may cause you to slack off and do a poor editing job.

Offering General Tips for Editing Technical Documents

Most technical writers complain that no one reads their documents. 'No one' usually refers to software developers and other subject matter experts. Writers are relatively cooperative. They'll gladly edit your work as long as you promise to return the favor. This isn't to imply that writers aren't busy. They just sympathize with you more because they know how hard it is to get their work edited.

In technical writing classes, you're told to submit your drafts with a cover sheet telling the reviewer to read the document and hand back their edits by a certain date. At most places I've worked, this practice is never used. Everyone is busy—developers, project managers, testers, writers, and whoever else is on the project.

So, how do you get people to read your stuff?

For starters, give them ample time. Don't give them two days to read a hundred-page manual. On the flip side, don't give them four weeks; they'll just toss your document on their desk and forget about it. A good time is one to two weeks.

Second, cajole them to read it. Tell the developers they owe you one because you found all those wonderful bugs. Tell your reviewers that the users are important and need correct information. If the users are dissatisfied, the product will fail, and you'll all be out of jobs. This is particularly true if you are writing documents for applications that will be sold in stores.

Third, for subject matter experts in particular, put revision bars next to those sections you have questions about and tell your reviewers to read just those sections. Do this for your first drafts, not just for subsequent drafts of your document. Your reviewers will love you because they won't have to wade through hundreds of pages.

Fourth, help your reviewers out by learning all you can about the subject. If you're documenting a mutual fund application, learn all you can about mutual funds. Go to the local library or bookstore and get a book on mutual funds. Get a dictionary of financial terms. The more you know, the fewer questions you have. The fewer questions you have, the fewer revision bars in the document and the less your reviewers will have to read.

Fifth, if you work on a team, have other writers check your document for style and grammar. If it's an end user document, have the writers check your procedures and conceptual material as well.

Finding Out about Contract Employment Agencies

For all of my technical writing jobs, I've worked as a contractor. Contractors are basically temporary workers. They work for a company for a limited time—weeks, months, or years—and then leave when the contract is up or the project is finished. Contractors can either work directly with the company or through a technical employment agency. On average, contractors make more money than full-timers, though they usually have to provide their own benefits. To work as a contractor, you need at least one year of experience.

I've contracted through agencies because it's easier. The agencies do the marketing for you. They already have the necessary contacts at several companies. When they find a job you're suited for, they give you call.

If you go through an agency, you'll make less money than if you contract directly with a company because the agency charges the company a fee, which can be anywhere from 10% to 50% or more of your hourly rate. If you're making $40 an hour, the agency's probably charging the company $50 or more per hour.

Even though agencies pay less, they are a good way to get contracts. If you hate drumming up business and trying to find new clients, you can let the agency do the work for you. All but two of my contracts have been through agencies, and I have never had a problem with them.

Finding Agencies

When you look for agencies, look for ones that specialize in placing technical writers. These agencies obviously will have the most technical writing jobs available. There are several ways to find agencies, including:

- Want ads. Buy the Sunday edition of any major paper in your area and start looking at the want ads. Inside, you may find the names of several agencies looking for technical writers.

- Phone book. Look under Employment Agencies, Employment Contractors, Personnel Agencies, Temporary Help Agencies, or Temporary Help Contractors.

- Society for Technical Communications (STC) publications. The STC produces two major publications, *intercom* and *Technical Communication*. Most agencies advertise in *intercom*.

- Other publications. Agencies also advertise in industry magazines, such as *Contract Professional*.

- Other contractors. Ask any contractors you know for referrals.

You need to contact all the agencies in your geographical area. There are at least two reasons why:

- Not all the agencies have jobs at the same time. If you limit yourself to just a few agencies, you may be missing out on other jobs at other agencies.

- Some companies have "preferred vendor" relationships with agencies. This means that the companies only work with a few agencies. If you're not listed with those agencies, you're out of luck.

After you contact an agency, a technical recruiter may call you. Most of the time the recruiter will tell you about a job opening. Other times, the recruiter will want to meet with you.

Meeting with a Recruiter

If you meet with a recruiter, you should bring along a copy of your résumé and portfolio. The recruiter will want to know what types of jobs you are looking for and what skills you like to use the most. They may ask you what type of working environment you like and the type of rate you expect. They may also ask to see samples of your work.

During the interview, you should ask the recruiter the following questions. Feel free to ask other questions as well.

- How long has the agency been in business?

    The longer an agency's been around, the more contacts and name recognition it will have.

- Does the agency get many calls for technical writers?

    Obviously, the more the better. You may also want to ask if the agency has any preferred vendor relationships with any companies.

- How often does the agency pay its contractors?

    Most agencies pay on a weekly basis; but some pay every two weeks.

- Does the agency offer any benefits?

    Some agencies offer insurance and retirement benefits to their contractors. Usually, though, you have to work for a year or more before you're eligible to get any benefits. But, it doesn't hurt to ask.

- Does the agency pay overtime?

You're considered a non-exempt employee because you get paid by the hour. So, supposedly, if you make less than six times the minimum wage, you're eligible for overtime pay, at one and one-half times your hourly rate. However, the law is a little fuzzy on this. If the agency doesn't pay it, just don't work overtime. Moreover, companies frown on contractors working overtime. Contractors cost the company enough money as it is.

- Does the agency give pay raises? If so, how often?

    Some agencies may give raises to their contractors, usually once a year.

- Can you work on a 1099 basis?

Most of the time, you will work with the agency as a W-2. This means you are essentially an employee of the agency. The agency will, therefore, be responsible for covering payroll taxes on your income.

As a 1099, you're responsible for paying your own taxes. The agency normally pays you a higher rate because you're doing the tax paperwork. However, fear of the IRS usually prevents agencies from hiring you as a 1099.

When an agency calls you about a job opening, ask these questions:

- Where is the job located?
- What it the length of the contract?
- What does the job entail?

Find out what you'll be doing. Ask what types of manuals you'll be writing and whether you'll be developing online help or building web pages, etc.

- What is the hourly rate?

Getting a Job Through an Agency

Before signing the contract, read it thoroughly, especially if it is your first job. Pay particular attention to the following areas:

- The hourly rate. Make sure it is the one you were quoted. If it's less, squawk.
- How often you get paid.
- The length of the contract. Make sure there's a specific start and end date.
- Whether the agency pays overtime.
- Whether the agency offers benefits, and if so, when you are eligible to receive them.
- Whether there is a non-compete clause, and if so, for how long. A non-compete clause states that if the company calls you back within a certain time frame (usually six months to one year) after your contract ends, you must contract through the agency. You cannot contract directly with the company or through another agency. Some contractors question the legality of these clauses, but most companies obey them anyway.

Most agencies use a standard contract, so after a while, you'll get to know all the clauses by heart. And feel free to have some clauses changed or to insert some of your own. If your suggestions are reasonable, the agency should oblige. I've never changed any contracts, and I've never run into any problems.

Looking in on a Day in the Life of a Technical Writer

If you're thinking of getting a job as a technical writer, you're probably wondering what the job is like. Surprisingly, you don't write eight hours a day, five days a week. You probably spend half your time writing. Most technical writers' days are split into the following tasks:

- Writing. You spend about half your time writing manuals. This may include creating a style sheet and formatting the document.

- Editing/Reading. You spend a good portion of your time reading and editing what you've written, particularly if you're the only writer on staff. If you work with a group of writers, you usually edit each other's work.

- Researching. When you start work on a project, it's a good idea to find any information that's been written up on it, such as development specifications. You also may find old manuals that were written for an earlier version of the product. Sales and marketing materials are also good sources of information.

- Application testing. If you're documenting an end-user product, you'll want to get a working prototype of the application. This way, you can start documenting how the application works. Your playing with the application will also help the programmers because you'll undoubtedly find bugs.

- Interviewing developers. As you're documenting an application, you'll run into roadblocks. You'll spend a good portion of your time searching for answers, but it's time well spent. After all, the more you know, the better you write. What's the best way to get in touch with a developer? For non-emergency questions, send them e-mail. For more pressing questions, you can call them or talk to them in person.

- Meetings. Yes, we all hate meetings, but some of them are actually worthwhile. If you can, sit in on the developer's meetings. These will give you an idea of where the application is heading. A lot of companies, still unaware of the importance of the writer, don't want you attend these meetings. Insist on going; the more you know, the better you write.

A lot of writers complain that they get no respect. They feel like they're the bottom rung on the ladder.

Unfortunately, a lot of companies agree with them. Granted, there are some companies that have teams of writers and editors and a formalized documentation process. These tend to be large companies with big budgets. Other companies have writers but no formal editing or documentation process. Still other companies hire no writers at all. They view them as irrelevant. "Why hire some literati from Princeton?" they say. "We'll just slap something together when we ship." A lot of small, start-up companies fall under this category.

Furthermore, software developers are busy people, and if you ask them dumb questions, they'll let you know. Think back to when you were in college. Who were the snobbiest students? The engineers. Well, guess what? You're working with them eight hours a day, five days a week. Don't reinforce their stereotype that you were an English major because you were too stupid to do anything else.

To gain more respect, branch out into other areas. Learn how to code. Develop an online help system. (You work closely with the developer when you do this. If you do a good job, you'll score points.) Do some software testing or build a website. Show that you have some technical knowledge.

The life of a technical writer isn't all roses. But if you learn to handle the rough spots, you'll gain the respect of your peers and become more valuable to the company.

• • •

Chapter 19.
Finding Time to Write

"What may be done at any time will be done at no time." Think about the truth of that Scottish proverb. If you put off doing what is important to you in favor of what everyone else needs or what everyone else thinks you should do, you are cheating yourself. If you tell yourself that you can do whatever you need any time and do all the other "stuff" first, you may never have the time to write. With a workable plan, though, you will be able to achieve your goals—personally, physically, emotionally, financially, and spiritually.

Achieving Positive Personal Performance in Six Steps

If you (1) plan your schedule with up-to-date to do lists, (2) prioritize time, people, and possessions, (3) write your purposes and goals, (4) control perfectionism, (5) overcome procrastination, and (6) check your progress, you are well on your way to more time for yourself and for your writing.

Taking Charge of Your Life

Taking charge of your life focuses your energy, nurtures your self concept, and reduces your stress. Planning and allocating is useful. Writing down your goals is even better toward helping you to achieve your goals. Your chances of following through are improved. Making uninterrupted block time available for yourself, for your writing, and for your chosen companions works wonders.

Lynn Grisard Fullman, the author of numerous books including *Alabama Family Adventure Guide, Alabama This Weekend*, and *Fun with the Family in Alabama*, says, "You have to make the time to write. You don't just happen upon it. You have to create a routine and, without excuse, stick with it. Adjust it if you need to, but keep writing, every day."

Passing Up That Ringing Phone

The telephone can be a perpetual interruption. Phone calls totally sidetrack some people. If this happens to you, you may decide to allow a telephone answering device or voice mail to take all your calls. Then you can consolidate and prioritize your return calls.

Prioritizing People

You may even decide to benefit yourself by prioritizing people. Give time only to the people whom you feel deserve your time and attention. If acquaintances are troubled, you can be compassionate, but they must find their own solutions. You can listen politely to their stories the first time. The next time, though, you may choose to acknowledge and honor them, but you can ask, "What are you going to do about that?" You will help to steer them toward seeking a solution or choosing a counselor to help rather than just fostering the replaying of their problem.

When someone invites you into a team project of any sort, make sure that the person is reliable and that the project has an excellent chance of fruition. Don't allow others to pull you away from your own work to engage in their projects unless you feel that you can benefit, too.

Parceling Out Excesses

Also, parceling out extraneous possessions from your life can help to clear some time for you. If there are "things" that you have outgrown your initial enchantment for and they get in your way or take your time, perhaps you can contribute them to Goodwill or the Salvation Army or some other organization of your choice.

Controlling Perfectionism

Make realistic demands on yourself and others. Strive for excellence, but know when to stop. Recognize when a project is finished. Accept finishing tasks without struggle. As it has been said before, "With perfection, there is no finish line."

Overcoming Procrastination

Avoid making excuses for delays in action toward your goals. Avoid waiting for the perfect time to begin your projects. Give yourself realistic deadlines, and set out to meet them. Divide potentially overwhelming projects into manageable mini tasks. Do the most difficult work first. Conquer it. Get it out of the way. Reward yourself when you finish.

Taking Time for Yourself

You will be rewarding yourself often as you adopt many of these guidelines. As a natural outcome, you also will find much more time for yourself, for your writing, and for those with whom you wish to share your life.

• • •

One of the most important tips when writing for an edition of an international brand is to study *THAT* edition, not to assume that, for example, because you are familiar with an American edition you will instantly understand the South African one. It's that new cliché: Think local; act global.

Vanessa Raphaely
COSMOPOLITAN
Cape Town, South Africa

All articles appearing in *WellBeing* are written by professionals in their fields or professional writers—without them we would not have a magazine.

Donna Welsh
WELLBEING
Sydney, NSW
Australia

It's all about presenting a professional package. Know your target magazine inside out. Only then can you hope to have any idea about what the editor is after. Then you can present a choice of original story ideas in clear, concise summaries, tailored to a specific section in a specific publication. Make it difficult for the editor to say no. If you were in his shoes, what would you want to see?

Paul Grogan
GLOBAL ADVENTURE
London, England

Chapter 20.
Fulfilling Your Dream

With the creation of *The Writer's Friend: Behind the Scenes with Editors*, it has been my aim to help prevent the collision courses that writers sometimes create for themselves when left to their own innocent devices. More than 40 editors and publishers from around the world and a powerful fistful of award-winning writers have shown how to get on the right track. They have explained how to find your dream publications, to know your audience, to know how to query, to maximize your research, and to improve your interviews. Words straight from the editors have illustrated how to capture an editor's attention. These editors and writers alike have contributed a cornucopia of ideas about how to find new twists for your articles and how to balance your communication.

After putting yourself in the shoes of Barry Wesson, Editor of *Show Horses* magazine, an editor whom Nancy McAlary and I have created, you can see that editors have lives, and families, and stresses, too, and you must observe natural laws of common sense and rules of etiquette when interacting with them. After peering over the shoulders of fictionalized writers Madison MacArthur and Rebecca Stanfield, you know whom to choose as your model, if you wish to succeed.

You now have a plethora of suggestions available to encourage your cooperation with editors. Let the suggestions presented in *The Writer's Friend* light your way through a dark and savage sea to success with editor after editor. Seek your auspicious direction. Remember that a principal secret to success lies in your attitude. Don't struggle. Don't argue. Don't fight with editors. Do your homework to find editors with whom you share common goals. When you do, you both can enjoy the voyage.

The bonus chapter, "Finding out about Editors, Employment Agencies, and Technical Writers," by Gregg introduces you to still another facet of writing to help you decide your direction.

Finally, *TWF* supplies a few tidbits to encourage you to find, take, or make the time to write, if, indeed, it is your dream to be a writer.

To make *The Writer's Friend* a user-friendly reference, I have collected the questions from the chapters and presented them in an appendix, "Questions to Help Focus Your Writing," and I have supplied an index.

I am grateful to you for having purchased *The Writer's Friend*, and I hope it helps you along your path to success as a writer. Keep it nearby as the champion of your cause. Remember, keep reading and writing and improving your work and believing in yourself to fulfill your dream. No matter what may try to keep you from your intended goal, if you persevere with discipline and submit your finest queries and best works, you will succeed.

Consider what Dan Auiler, author of *Vertigo: The Making of a Hitchcock Classic* and *The Hitchcock Notebooks*, tells his beginning screenwriters, "Write. Dream. Write. And try not to care that the people reading your work seldom give it the time it deserves. Endure. That's always Shakespeare's advice. Endure."

Happy writing!

· · ·

Editor's Note

Persistence is not merely repeating the same set of actions with the hope of one day miraculously finding success. It involves a critical assessment of those actions and the willingness to change one's course, if need be.

If it is your dream to write and to be published, but rejections dash your hopes, do not give up. From my personal experience as an editor, I can tell you that a rejection is less a disparagement of the writer's creative ability than the writer's marketing habits. The secret lies in finding your market, and to that end Kyle has surveyed literally dozens of editors from around the world to discover the best way to help you do this.

Editor after editor has confirmed that writers make similar mistakes when dealing with editors, and they lay bare what they do not like about writers' attitudes, habits, and submissions. This book is more than a collection of interviews with different editors—it is a blueprint for building profitable relationships with editors that will last your entire writing career.

There is a Chinese proverb that says, "If you give a man a fish, you feed him for a day. If you teach a man to fish, you feed him for his lifetime." *The Writer's Friend* is a guide to building the necessary skill of marketing your writing in the publishing industry. While differences in topics and essence of presentation do, indeed, naturally exist from publication to publication, you can discover how to recognize those important differences by studying this book. Once learned, this skill will serve you as long as you continue writing.

The Writer's Friend can help you, but you must put into practice what it shares. Only then can it work for you. Let this peek behind the scenes with editors speed you along your path to becoming a writer whose works editors welcome again and again.

Guy Lancaster
Editor, *The Writer's Friend*

Appendix.
Questions to Help
Focus Your Writing

Chapter 2. Getting on the Right Track

Take time to explore each of your target publications. Ask yourself questions you may not have asked yourself ever before as a "reader" of the magazine.

- Do all the articles in your target magazine nab the reader's attention and thrust toward a single big picture?
- Do the articles supply a potpourri of ideas?
- Can you determine the mission of your target market?
- Does your target publication pride itself on testing the products that it advertises and attempting to review those products without bias?
- Can you determine the goal of your target magazine?
- Is your target publication service-oriented?
- Does your target publication primarily educate or primarily entertain?
- Do your own personal attitudes coincide with the values of your target publication?
- Are you on the same wavelength with your target publication?

One way to test yourself is to note whether or not you are a user of the products the magazine advertises.

- Do special theme issues come out seasonally or annually?
- Do the topics cluster around people, animals, places, products, or qualities?
- Does every issue feature a famous person or teach about a rare bird or warn of political crisis?
- Does every issue give information about caring for your exotic automobile?
- Does every issue give information about new FDA rulings?

- Does every issue whisk you to a honeymoon hideaway or pioneer a colorful new product?
- Does every issue scrutinize qualities like love, fear, anger, or jealousy?
- Do the titles take the same structural form throughout the magazine?
- Are all the titles brief?
- Are titles and subtitles used?
- Are the titles given in the form of a question?
- Do the titles startle the reader?

Chapter 3. Finding Your Dream Publications

Learning from Your Writer Friends

- Have your writer friends written for your dream market?
- Did your dream magazine permit simultaneous queries or simultaneous submissions of typescripts?
- Did your writer friends receive a fair contract with terms spelled out clearly?
- Was the contract sent promptly?
- How did their assignments go?
- How well did their communications with the editor go?
- How soon did they learn of their acceptance?
- Were they promised payment on acceptance?
- Were they to be paid upon publication?
- Were the editor's instructions clear?
- Were they asked to do rewrites? If so, was the editor helpful and clear with instructions?
- Did the editor call for an entirely new piece because of a change in his plans? If so, did he increase their compensation?
- If the editor rewrote any large portions of their work, did the editor ask their approval and give them the opportunity to withdraw the story?
- Did the editor want any local or regional acquaintances, political, or social figures stuffed into the article or touted?
- Did the editor want advertisers plugged?

- How soon were their pieces published?
- Were their works published with care?
- Did the editorial staff butcher the names of any of their experts or leave out the experts' affiliation, thus causing problems for your writer friends with that noteworthy person?
- When the editor was asked to print a correction, did he follow through with a correction? Or did he ignore your writer friends and leave them to deal with the expert's hurt feelings?
- Were they pleased with illustrations that the editor added?
- Did the illustrations accurately complement their text?
- Did the writers supply illustrations or photographs?
- What rights to their transparencies or photographs were purchased?
- Did they receive extra compensation for their photography?
- Were photographs required as part of the assignment, but without additional compensation for the photos?
- Were they given a byline for their photographs?
- How much were they paid for their articles?
- How promptly did their checks arrive?
- Have your writer friends built a long-standing relationship with the editor?
- Do they feel a loyalty to the editor and wish to continue the special writer-editor partnership?

Thinking about What Draws You to Your Target Market

- Are you clear about the scope and tone of the magazine?
- Why does this magazine have loyal readers?
- What intrigues you as a reader? If you can flip through the magazine without ever being captured by an intriguing title or topic, other readers may also.
- Can you hardly put away the magazine once you begin reading? Why? What mesmerizes you?
- Do you read article after article eagerly?
- Can you see your service article building on the information shared in this month's service article?
- Can you write an article that you feel could replace an article in your target magazine?

Exploring More Specific Target Publications

Study the last 12 to 24 issues of your target magazine or newspaper.

- Are the pieces in the form of interviews, or are they merely straight narrative?
- Does each issue have a theme?
- Are queries required, or does the editor prefer that completed typescripts be submitted?
- Can you supply a needed story?
- If your target journal or magazine documents materials, which style sheet is followed?
- Study the photographs. Does the editor require that photos accompany your article?
- Does the editor want color transparencies or black and white photos?
- Can you supply color transparencies with excellent composition to give your sports story an edge?
- Can you supply black and white photographs to support your story?

If you wish to be published in a literary journal, then read and study an ample number of issues to get a feel for the writing styles the editors appreciate and the themes they embrace.

- Are the titles long or short?
- Are the titles posed as questions?
- Are titles and subtitles used?
- Are headings and subheadings used in the body of the text of every article or story?
- Can you write on a suitable topic for the magazine?
- Does your genre and style fit the magazine?

Chapter 4. Knowing Your Audience

Check the pulse of your target publication. Write down your impressions of the magazine's cover and its articles.

- Does the cover catch your eye? If so, why?
- Can you recognize the magazine by its cover?
- What makes that publication unique?

To learn about your audience, study the feature articles very closely. Ask yourself the following questions.

- What intrigues the readers?
- What keeps them buying the magazine?
- Are the readers loyal for many years, or do they outgrow their need for the magazine?
- Are the articles features, essays, or reports?
- Are they service oriented?
- Do the articles educate?
- What level of expertise must the reader already have about the topic to understand the articles presented?
- Do the articles and stories entertain?
- Are the articles photo-driven?
- Are the illustrations or photos so excellent they almost tell the story without text?
- What is the publication's mission?
- Do the articles presented in the magazine seem to have only one voice?
- Can you detect numerous individual writer's voices?
- What concerns do the readers have?

For several days think about what you have discovered. Then study all of those issues again. Write down your impressions of the covers and the articles.

- Have your impressions changed?
- What insights do you feel you now have that you did not have upon your first study?

Chapter 5. Preparing to Query

Think through some useful questions to guide your preparation.

- What new information will you be able to share with readers?
- How will the information impact their lives?
- What lead time are you considering for your article?
- What is the lead time of your target publication? Keeping in mind the magazine's anticipated response time, can you match its lead time effectively?

- From the day of your go-ahead, how much time will you need to prepare your piece and have it in your editor's hands? When you make your promise, give yourself some buffer time to cover emergencies.

- Does your target publication prefer postal submissions or e-mail submissions?

- Is your publication local, regional, national, or international? If the editor does not permit e-mail submissions, you must remember to take into consideration the location of the publisher and give ample time for the postal service or use overnight delivery services. In any event, plan to meet your deadline in advance, if possible. It will make your editor happy to receive your work a bit early.

- Do you feel confident that you can develop your article in accordance with the word limit of your target publication?

- Do you feel confident about your research findings and potential contributions from experts you will interview?

- Have you written other articles on other aspects of your topic?

Chapter 6. Composing a Sparkling Query Letter

Self-Editing Your Query

Become "the editor," and ask yourself these questions about "the writer" of the query. Remain as objective as you can. Get rid of any errors that have sneaked into your work.

- Has "this writer" confined the query to a single page? It is important to keep the query to the standard single page. A succinct query shows a great deal about how well you can handle materials.

- Has "this writer" typed absolutely correctly the name and address of the specific editor to whom the work should go?

- Has "this writer" offered a specific article for sale, and does it match its target market?

- Do you—as the editor you now are role-playing—like what you see? If not, why? Mark the corrections that must be made to improve the work.

- Does the text appear aesthetically pleasing?

- Does the cotton bond paper and your mono-spaced font present a clean image?

- Are your margins at least one to one and one-half inches on all sides?
- Is the beginning sentence clear and captivating?
- Does the query intrigue you?
- Can you read "this writer's" letter with ease?
- Are the grammar, spelling, and punctuation in this letter correct, and are they conveyed in an appropriate tone?
- Are the paragraphs well-developed, yet succinct?
- Do you know which experts or celebrities "the writer" will interview?
- Do you sense a spirit of cooperation and confidence from the words of "this writer"?
- What special insight or experience does "this writer" possess that will make this article one to remember?
- Will your audience want to read "this writer's" article?
- Why is "this writer" the perfect candidate for this particular article?
- Do you know what the query proposes and how "the writer" plans to handle the preparation of the article?
- Why will "this writer's" work impact the reader?
- Does "this writer" know the word limit?
- Will "this writer" supply photos?
- Will "this writer" supply a sidebar?
- How soon will "this writer" complete the article?
- Does "this writer" supply clips?
- After reading "this writer's" query and thinking through these questions and others that may come to mind, answer this question, Would you assign this topic to "this writer"?

Chapter 8. Interviewing and Beyond

You will know that your research is complete and that your work is finished when you fit all your puzzle pieces together into your article.

- Does your article say what you had intended?
- Does it inform?
- Does it entertain?

- Does it inspire?
- Does it touch a nerve?
- Does it haunt you as you go about your day?
- Will it linger in the minds of your readers, too?

After you complete your practice interview, think about the following questions.

- Were you well prepared to conduct your interview?
- Were your questions succinct?
- Were your questions clear?
- Were your questions too wordy?
- Did you talk too much?
- Did you give your interviewee ample time to speak?
- Were you listening closely?
- Did you rush in too soon with your next prepared question?
- Were you flexible so that you could follow up on important unanticipated aspects that your interviewee introduced?
- Were you quiet at the right moments?
- Did you avoid asking questions that could be answered merely with a yes or no?
- When you did not get the answer you wanted, did you come back to it later and ask it in a different way that was clearer to your interviewee? If so, what do you feel blurred the first version of your question?
- Were you persistent without being pushy or overbearing?
- Were you able to extract exciting quotes to spice up your article?
- Were you able to focus on the aspect of your article that you chose to develop?
- Did you maintain control of the interview?
- At the end of the interview, did you offer time for your interviewee to speak about something of interest that you perhaps had overlooked asking?

Chapter 9. Improving Your Style

Self-Editing Your Nonfiction

Ask yourself the following questions.

Regarding Your Introduction

- Is your introduction captivating enough to keep your readers reading?
- Do you get right to the point then guide your reader quickly down a well-marked path?
- What is the purpose of your article?
- Why is your material important?
- Why are you the best person to write this article?

Regarding Your Composition

- Is your article organized and developed in a logical order?
- Are steps missing that the reader needs in order to understand your information?
- Do you stay true to your goal, or do you wander off course, losing your bewildered reader who flips to the next article or tosses the magazine?
- Do you include information that intrigues you but does not fit in properly with the remaining material? If so, as difficult as it may seem, you must get rid of excesses.
- Do bullets or numbers help you to enumerate your story's salient presentation?
- Do you choose words that have the best tone for your subject matter?
- Do you employ vigorous verbs in active voice?
- Do you maintain a consistent verb tense?
- Do you use too many adjectives, or do you follow Mark Twain's advice in *Pudd'nhead Wilson*, "As to Adjectives: when in doubt, strike it out"?
- Will your words be understood easily by their intended audience?
- Are your sentences of varied lengths to prevent a choppy read?
- Are your sentences so long they cannot be read in one breath?

- Do your sentences have a pleasant rhythm? Read your article aloud and listen to its words and their cadence. Have you chosen powerful and melodious words?
- Do you give specific details that engage the senses of your readers and make your piece memorable from well-drawn images?

Have someone read your work aloud to you. Close your eyes and listen.

- In your mind's eye, as you listen, do your words show bursts of crimson and azure?
- Do you smell the fragrance of magnolias or the aroma of fresh baked brioche?
- Do you hear the lonesome moan of the midnight train?

- Must you dodge windswept leaves?
- Do you feel the chill from the blast of a sudden cold front?
- Are your sentences drab and flat?

Regarding Your Conclusion
- Will your conclusion linger in the minds of your readers, or is it merely a rehash of what you already have offered?

Chapter 12. Controlling Your Inner Editor

Editing Your Own Work

In General—Ask Yourself
- Does the title titillate its readers?
- Is the title suitable to the work and to its target market?
- Does your opening sentence entice the reader and hold attention?

About Your Story—Ask Yourself
- Is your story the right genre for your target market?
- Will enough readers relate to your story to want to read it, or is its theme too specialized?
- Does the story develop in a believable fashion?
- Does the theme of your story build logically?

- Does your chain of incidents link together in the most powerful order?
- Is your setting clear?
- Is the immediacy or time limit of your story short enough to make and keep the story suspenseful?
- Does the plot of your story unfold dramatically and hold the reader's attention?
- Do you keep your story flowing with the just right details?
- Are your characters well drawn?
- Can you feel each character's pain or joy?
- Do your characters speak with convincing dialogue?
- Are there sufficient conflicts and challenges for the protagonist to overcome?
- Do you have an endearing positive supporting character or characters and an unforgettable antagonist?
- Is the tone that you want in your story developed and maintained or changed as you desired?
- Does your story have a beginning, a middle, and an end?
- Does your story capture your reader's attention?
- Does your story impact the reader?
- Does your story linger in the mind of the reader?

About Your Article—Ask Yourself

Introduction

- Will your opening sentence intrigue your readers?
- Do you stay on your topic or wander away and lose your reader?
- Is your slant appropriate for your target market?
- Are there sufficient eager readers who want to learn about your topic?
- Is the sale of your article supported by a market willing to purchase the magazine?
- Do you set your intended tone early?

Composition

- Can you meet your readers' needs with a suitable breadth and depth of information?

- Do you offer enough new and useful information to merit publication?
- Are your points organized in a meaningful order so that your work flows?
- Are your points well substantiated?
- Is your message sharply focused, or do you wander and add extraneous information that is enchanting to you but is intrusive in this particular article?
- Do you use too many words to make your points?
- Do you use the best words to convey your meaning?
- Do you use active voice?
- Do you use action verbs?
- Do you maintain verb tense?
- Do you paint a vivid image that your reader can see?
- Can your reader hear, feel, smell, and touch what you bring to life through your words?
- Are your words compelling?
- Do you convey your message in a way that entices the reader to keep reading?
- Do you mesmerize your reader?
- Can you tighten up some sentences and delete some others to improve the readability of your article?
- Are any sentences scattered that should be brought together for greater clarity?
- Are repetitious sentences marring your article? If so, you can delete the ones that are ineffective or modify both and weave them together for finer detail.
- Can you rearrange a paragraph here and there to smooth the flow of your piece?
- Are your transitions smooth?
- Are anecdotes used in other articles in your target magazine? If so, can you use anecdotes to help convey your message?
- Do you give useful examples and extrapolations to guide your readers?
- Do you have quotes from authorities on both sides of the issue you are explaining?

- Have you met or exceeded your editor's word limit for your article?
- Have you successfully conveyed the who, what, when, where, why, and how about your topic?

Conclusion

- Does your conclusion wrap up your article well?
- Have you acknowledged your sources either in the text or as footnotes or following the body of your text, according to your editor's preference?
- Have you noted personal communication sources following the text?
- Do you maintain the tone that you set out to create in your piece?
- Does your tone change as you intended?
- Finally, ask yourself, have you entertained, surprised, astonished, or informed your reader with the information in your article?

Chapter 14. Balancing Your Communication

Study the tone of the articles in your target publication, and ask yourself the following questions.

- Do the articles show divergent viewpoints from opposing experts?
- Do you feel confident to handle the material for your article objectively?
- Will you be able to show both sides of an issue in the allotted word limit?
- Can you supply materials from your own experience and from other resources and interviewees?
- Do the bulk of the articles rely on statements from authorities in their fields, or are the majority of the articles written by experts on their topics?
- What are the customs of the readers?
- What approximate age are the readers?
- What are the locations of the readership of your target magazine?

Chapter 16. Finding a New Twist

Thinking about Conversations People Share with You

- What is of compelling interest to your friends around the world?
- What did the airline passenger next to you have to say?
- What interests your tennis partner?
- What catches your hairstylist's attention?
- What did your supermarket clerk mention to you?
- When is your friend's next bridge tournament?
- What triggered a conversation with your child's orthodontist?

Thinking of Travel Ideas

- What city, state, or country did you just visit?
- Where will you be traveling next?

Thinking about Your Own City

Unique Qualities

- What is unique about your city? What is its main calling card?
- Why would visitors want to visit your city?
- Why is your city or state a leader in recycling, sock making, peach growing, guitar making, or some other topic that an editor would find appealing for his particular audience?
- Why is your city known especially for its volunteer spirit?
- Why has the crime rate of your city diminished during the last year?
- What can you say about your city's unique qualities?
- Why is your town supercharged or sleepy regarding politics?
- What forces lead your city?
- What special goals does your city have?
- Why is your city constantly astir with conventions?
- What special ways does your city have to prevent or handle pollution?
- Why is your city teeming with new industry?
- Which businesses are most prominent?
- What new ordinances are being put in place?

- How does your city nurture families and children?
- Why is your city a vacation spot for visitors?
- What brings the most revenue to your city?

Professions and Hobbies

- How many professions are represented in your town?
- How many different kinds of health care professions—traditional and complementary—are represented in your city?
- How is your city positively impacted by its university or universities?
- How is your town negatively impacted if it has no universities?
- How many art galleries and museums are in your city?
- Which museum is your city's oldest and finest?
- How long has a unique bootmaker, swordmaker, or candy kitchen been in your city?
- How many computer businesses are in your city?
- Who among your friends have interesting collections?
- What hobbies or recreational activities are represented by clubs and organizations in your city—gardening, quilting, knitting, boat making, touring, kayaking, spelunking, mountain climbing, repelling, or bungee jumping?

Thinking about Personalities in Your City

- Who is the youngest or oldest doctor, lawyer, pharmacist, naturopath, or acupuncturist in your city?
- Who are your favorite athletes? Interview them.
- What are your neighbor's unique talents?

Entertainment

- Which sports are your favorites?
- How many fitness centers thrive in your city?
- How many golf courses does your city boast?
- How does your racetrack impact your city's economy?
- Why is your city a leader in pet shows?
- When is the next rodeo coming to your town?

- Where can you go in your town to take horseback riding lessons?
- What games enchant your children?
- Which holidays reverberate with activity in your city?
- Would your city's calendar of events enthrall readers? Where? Why? Which publication would be interested in which event?
- Which magazines are published in your city?

Food

- Who among your friends is a wine connoisseur?
- Who among your friends is a gourmet cook?
- What favorite recipes can you or your club share?

Purchases

- Do you have special budgeting tips you can offer?
- Can you write about your time-saving shopping tips?

Chapter 18. Finding out about Editors, Agents, and Technical Writers

By Joseph Gregg

During the interview, you should ask the recruiter the following questions.

- How long has the agency been in business?
- Does the agency get many calls for technical writers?
- How often does the agency pay its contractors?
- Does the agency offer any benefits?
- Does the agency pay overtime?
- Does the agency give pay raises? If so, how often?
- Can you work on a 1099 basis?
- Where is the job located?
- What it the length of the contract?
- What does the job entail?
- What is the hourly rate?

Index

Fictional Personalities from "A Day in the Life of an Editor"

Printed Matter—Subjects

Printed and Web Material—Sources

ASJA Code of Ethics and Fair Practices. *American Society of Journalists and Authors 1999 Membership Directory*. New York: ASJA, Inc., 1999.

ASJA "Contract tips: Electronic rights in newspaper and magazine contracts."
<http://www.asja/org/asjatips.htm>

ASJA "Contract tips: Watch out for these clauses."
<http://www.asja/org/asjaclauses.htm>

The Gila Queen's Guide to Markets 86 (Spring 1997).
[*The Beloit Poetry Journal*]

Irving, Washington. *Tales of a Traveller. Bracebridge Hall, Tales of a Traveller,* and *The Alhambra*. New York: The Library of America, 1991.

Kyle, Davis. "Warm Up for a Smart Start." *Balance Fitness* (May 1996), 3 pp.
<http://balance.net/balance/96/1_5/fitness/exercise/warmup.htm>

Kyle, Linda Davis. "Enjoy a Pest-Free Haven."
Maryland Maturity Lifestyles (June 1996), 38+.

_____. "Planning a Great Holiday Party." *Tradewind* (Winter 1995), 10–12.

_____. "Shoe-Shopping Tips from the AOFAS." *BodyIsland*
3 June 1999, 2 pp.
<http://www.bodyisland.com/feature/shoe-shopping.htm>

Marston, Ralph S., Jr. "Details." *The Daily Motivator* 13 May 1999.
<http://greatday.com/motivate/990517.html>

Russell, Bertrand. "How I Write." *Portraits from Memory*. New York: Simon & Schuster, 1963.

_____. *Sceptical Essays*. New York: W.W. Norton & Company, Inc., 1928.

Twain, Mark. *Pudd'nhead Wilson*. *Mississippi Writings: The Adventures of Tom Sawyer, Life on the Mississippi, Adventures of Huckleberry Finn,* and *Pudd'nhead Wilson*. New York: The Library of America, 1982.

West, Jessamyn. *Hide and Seek: A Continuing Journey*. New York: Harcourt Brace Jovanovich, 1973.

Williams, Roger J. *Rethinking Education: The Coming Age of Enlightenment*. New York: Philosophical Library, 1986.

The Write Markets Report (February 1998), 11. [Mobility]

Contributors to *The Writer's Friend*

Altair
www.ozemail.com.au/~robsteph/agency.htm

American Society of Journalists and Authors
www.asja.org

The Arkansas Review: A Journal of Delta Studies
www.clt.astate.edu/arkreview

Bahrain Gateway, Golden Falcon, Oryx, Oryx—Entertainment

Balance Fitness
[predecessor of *BodyIsland*]

BodyIsland
www.bodyisland.com

CATsumer Report and *Good Dog!*
www.prodogs.com/dmn/gooddog/index.htm

CC Motorcycle NewsMagazine
www.moto-mag.com/

Continental
www.continental.com/

Cosmopolitan
www.cosmopolitan.co.za/

The Diamond Angle
www.aloha.net/~tdaflow/

The Educated Traveler
www.educated-traveler.com/

Estylo

The First Word Bulletin
www.interlink.es/peraso/first/

Gila Queen's Guide to Markets
www.gilaqueen.com/

Global Adventure
www.globaladventuremag.com/

Great Lakes Angler
www.glangler.com/

The Greyhound Review
http://nga.jc.net

Healthy Options

Homes & Cottages
www.homesandcottages.com/

Inklings, Inkspot's Newsletter for Writers
www.inkspot.com and www.inkspot.com/inklings/

International Railway Traveler
www.trainweb.com/irtsociety/

Italian America
www.osia.org/

Jewish Affairs

Lakeland Boating
www.lakelandboating.com/

Massage Magazine
www.massagemag.com/

Model Railroader
http://www.kalmbach.com/

Nature
www.nature.com/

NEWSdesk
www.profnet.com/
www.newsdesk.com/

News-Record

Notre Dame Magazine
www.nd.edu/~ndmag/

Persimmon Hill
www.cowboyhalloffame.org/

Popular Communications
www.popcomm.com/

PR NewsWire
www.prnewswire.com

PRN Press Room
www.prnmedia.com

Professional Counselor Magazine
www.professionalcounselor.com

Sailing
www.sailnet.com/sailing/

San Francisco Peninsula Parent
family.go.com/Local/sfpn/

Sci-Fi Entertainment
www.ncbuy.com/magazines/1161.html

The Silver Web

U.S. Art

Vista Magazine
www.vistamagazine.com/

Weekend Woodcrafts
www.weekendwoodcrafts.com/

WellBeing
www.wellbeing.com.au

The Write Markets Report
www.writersmarkets.com/

Selected Contributors to *WritingNow.com*

Courtesy of *WritingNow.com*

• **Features and/or "Writers around the World"**

Dan Auiler, Author of *Vertigo: The Making of a Hitchcock Classic* and *The Hitchcock Notebooks*, Los Angeles, CA

Liz Carpenter, Author of *Ruffles and Flourishes*, *Getting Better All the Time*, and *Unplanned Parenthood*, Austin, TX

Ron Franscell, Editor of *News Record* and Author of *Angel Fire* and *The Deadline*, Gillette, WY

Sonia Pressman Fuentes, Author of *Eat First—You Don't Know What They'll Give You*, Potomac, MD
www.1stbooks.com

Lynn Grisard Fullman, Columnist and Author of *Alabama Family Adventure Guide*, *Alabama This Weekend*, and *Fun with the Family in Alabama*, Birmingham, AL

Joseph Gregg, Author of *Write Your Way to Riches*, Methuen, PA
writeformoney.hypermart.net

Michael Levine, Author of *Triangle of Death*,
(Co-Author Laura Kavanau-Levine)
Stone Ridge, NY
Fight Back idt.net/~dorisaw/FightBack/

Ralph Marston, Author of *The Daily Motivator*, Austin, TX
www.greatday.com

Nancy McAlary, SS Romance Author, Has been featured in *Woman's Day*,
The People's Friend, *New Idea*, Brisbane, Queensland, Australia

Margaret McAlister, Author of *Be Seen, Get Known, Move Ahead*,
Shellharbour, NSW, Australia

Fern Michaels, Author of over 70 Romance Novels, Summerville, SC
fernmichaels.com/

Debbie Ridpath Ohi, Author/Editor of *Inklings*,
Inkspot's Newsletter for Writers, Toronto, Ontario, Canada
www.inkspot.com and www.inkspot.com/inklings/

Robert Powers, Columnist and Co-Author of *Satan Hunter*, Marietta, OH

Robert J. Sawyer, Author of a dozen SF books including *Factoring
Humanity* and *Flashforward* and winner of the 1995 Nebula Award and 20
other national and international writing awards, Thornhill, Ontario, Canada
www.sfwriter.com/

Shara Rendell-Smock, Author of *Getting Hooked* and *Living with Big Cats*
www.geocities.com/Athens/Agora/2859/

• **Letters to the Editor**
Courtesy of *WritingNow.com*

B. Adams
Adib
Melissa Anderson
Owen Court
Denise

James Floto
Rita Jette
L. Moore
K. Moriarty
Kim Baldwin Radford

Comments from Readers of *WritingNow.com*

From Australia —

An Invaluable Resource

I have found *WritingNow.com* to be an invaluable resource. Keep up the good work!

Kim Baldwin Radford
Sydney, NSW, Australia

From California —

So Many Ideas and So Much Hope

I think your newsletter is great. You have given me so many ideas and so much hope that my head is spinning! Keep it up!

K. Moriarty
Lake Forest, CA

From Canada —

Nuts and Bolts of Getting Published

I have just finished reading your "Knowing What an Editor Wants." I found it very informative. All of the information is presented thoroughly in a clear, well-arranged manner. I'm certainly going away from your page feeling like I have a grasp on the nuts and bolts of getting published.

Owen Court
Vancouver, BC, Canada

From Hawaii —

Great Material for the Working Writer!

Aloha,

Thank you very much for the fine online writing publication, *WritingNow.com*. I enjoy it so much I don't even bother with *Writer's Digest* anymore. Your material is much better for the working writer.

James Floto, Editor/Publisher
The Diamond Angle
www.aloha.net/~tdaflow
Kihei, HI

From Malaysia —
Thank You

Just to let you know, I am a subscriber of your e-zine from Kuala Lumpur, Malaysia. Thank you very much for a very informative e-zine.

Adib
Kuala Lumpur, Malaysia

From Michigan —
Great Service

Hello Linda,

What a great service to freelance writers! Keep up the good work. You are to be commended for a great and resourceful website!

Denise
Monroe, MI

From Missouri —
Good Tips

Just had my first issue and enjoyed it very much. Very good tips and timely articles.

B. Adams
Springfield, MO

From Rhode Island —
Terrific Website

Linda,

I think your site is terrific. I'm a new (late bloomer) writer, and I really appreciate your site. I'm full of questions, so it is great to find answers and advice that are well-written.

Thanks much,
Rita Jette
Cranston, RI

From Tasmania —
Great Stuff!

As a budding author, I've enjoyed your hints and recommendations for writers. Great stuff.

L.Moore
Tasmania

From Texas —
Interesting Writing

I was so excited to find your magazine on the internet. Let me guess—99 percent of all your e-mails begin that way. I took college creative writing two semesters ago, and I found myself fired up to write; but when the class ended, I was quite at a loss as to what to do with myself. I had no great professor to give me tips or edit my journal entries or say this is promising—nothing. Now, God has opened up the floodgates of heaven and rained down intelligible, practical help.

Merci,
Melissa Anderson
Houston, TX

ORDERING INFORMATION

Domestic and International Secure Visa/Master Card Orders:

www.writingnow.com

Prepay Mail Orders:

Domestic Orders

Post your name and address along with your Money Order or Check in US funds made payable to WritingNow.com Publishing. Add Shipping & Handling by US Priority Mail US$3.95 for first book (US$2.00 for each additional book). Texas residents add 8.25 % Sales Tax.

WritingNow.com Publishing
P.O. Box 270070
Austin, TX 78727

The Writer's Friend: Behind the Scenes with Editors	US$ 14.95
Shipping & Handling	US$ 3.95
Total	US$ 18.90

• • •

International Orders

Post your name and address along with your Money Order or Check in US funds *only* made payable to WritingNow.com Publishing. Add US$5.00 per book for shipping by international airmail outside the United States.

WritingNow.com Publishing
P.O. Box 270070
Austin, TX 78727
USA

The Writer's Friend: Behind the Scenes with Editors	US$ 14.95
International Airmail outside the United States and Handling	US$ 5.00
Total	US$ 19.95

Please include your e-mail address so that we may contact you about your order, if necessary. Thank you.

Thank you for your order!